D1825633

The Shellacking

The Obama Presidency,
the Tea Party, and the
2010 midterm elections

_____

Guy Rundle

K-_ist_ BOOKS

First published by K-ist Books 2010
© Guy Rundle 2010
All rights reserved

The moral rights of this author have been asserted

K-ist
124/77 Beak St, London, W1F 9DB

www.kistbooks.com

to Geoff Sharp, who taught me how to think

Contents

introduction

I'm not recommending for every future president that
they take a shellacking like they...like I did last night...
Barack Obama, November 3, 2010

More than sixty House of Representatives seats lost, six Senate seats, eight governorships and at least six hundred state seats...the 2010 United States midterm elections will live in the historical memory as one of the more stunning rebukes to a President and his administration. Two years after Barack Obama won election by an eight-state margin, on an unashamedly liberal programme, millions of voters either refused to re-endorse his party, or switched their support to a Republican party that had gone further to the Right than at any time in its history. The Republican leadership in Congress, and their supporters in the media, trumpeted loud and long that this was not merely a repudiation of Obama and his policies, but an affirmative vote for lower tax, smaller government and a 'return to the Constitution', and nothing else.

This was easy to refute, but establishing the real and mixed motives behind the 2010 vote was less straightforward. Did it indicate a dual effect, a combination of an attack from the right angered by the administration's mildly liberal programmes, together with a refusal of support by people who felt their demand for a genuinely left-progressive social programme had been denied? How much of it was due to independent voters who blamed the administration, fairly or otherwise, for the lack of consensus government in Washington? And how much of it was pure protest, an anti-political oppositionality, or a contradictory vote, a demand for both deficit reduction, lower taxes *and* job creation? Trying to determine the complex moods of the American people, and the changing ways in which media, class, neighbourhood, workplace and other factors were shaping political thinking and party loyalties was one key focus in these elections.

For leftists and progressives there was another, supplementary inquiry to be made, and that was concerning the aims and strategy of the Obama administration and the Pelosi-Reid Congressional majority, as well as their ultimate character. The administration's early decision to rehire many of the Wall Street insiders who had run Treasury prior to the 2008 crash, together with the relatively mild stimulus package, the early abandonment of the public option in healthcare, and the non-pursuit of the Employee Free Choice Act, had split progressives down the middle, dividing those who thought that the administration was practising the art of the possible under conditions of great difficulty, from those who believed it had been easily spooked, or that it had never had any real desire to prosecute a serious progressive agenda in the first place. The administration and the leaders in Congress could point to the fact that their majority was grounded on representatives who had been elected from Republican districts; they could highlight the power and autonomy of the 'Blue Dogs' coalition drawn from members largely elected from those demographics; they could point to the power given to individual Blue Dog Democratic senators by the de facto filibuster-proof supermajority now required for most government business. Finally they could point to the 1994 healthcare bill defeat in the first Clinton term, as a reason to hedge and trim and gain victories that could be pointed to. Those arguing against this view claimed that much of this reasoning was false, and that the situations did not compare, that Obama's confirmation vote had been huge, and that the Democratic party could be whipped into line if required. The failure to do so was evidence, they said, either of poor judgement, or of a lack of desire to make real categorical change in the first place.

By the time that this debate was underway among progressives, the national mood had changed decisively, and the Obama mantra of 'hope and change', and 'we are the people we have been waiting for' had been superseded by a new and quite different trend, which gave rose to the Tea Party. Whether they are a real movement at all is a question that is explored in these pages; but the very fact of their presence changed the whole political-cultural framework. This sudden rise to prominence of a political myth connecting to the deepest channels of American history transformed the election from one focused on the limits and possibilities of progressivism, to a case study in the role of idea, image and money in the formation of values and beliefs.

This made the election of great interest in itself – and makes also some attempt to understand what went on vital for progressives across the board from mainstream American liberals, through social democrats, to those who believe that a more categorical transformation is possible. This volume is a small contribution to that, drawn from reports written for the Australian politics daily Crikey.com.au, the *Sunday Age* (Melbourne) and the *Canberra Times*. It is intended as an immediate report with some pro-tem interpretation rather than a deeper study, with some attempt to match American political processes to cultural shifts which are not always apparent to Americans themselves. American readers may find some of this overexplicative for a foreign audience; non-American readers may find some sections on the baroque byways of American political institutions overly opaque. Thus I hope there is something to confuse everybody. There are several people to thank: Sophie, Jason and all at Crikey in Australia, Mary-Anne at *The Age*, Gillian at the *Canberra Times*, Vic Fingerhut, Sidney Blumenthal, Jim Newell, Alan Mascarenhas, Don Watson, Keli Carender, Nicholas Johnston in Iowa, Laurie Couch, Sandy Dailey, Hayden Schortman at the SEIU, Harley Dennett, Derek Shearer, Kaz 'Daily', among others. Above all Jess, for making me do it right. All mistakes are my own, or Nancy Pelosi's.

Portland, Maine, November 2010

1.

September 2010. The story so far...

By the first part of 2010, it was clear that Barack Obama and the Democratic Party were in some trouble, politically. Since taking office in January 2009, with an approval rating of more than sixty per cent, the country's first African-American President had suffered a continuous slide in regard and support, amid a series of major challenges, many of which he had not anticipated in planning a comprehensive reform programme. Chief among them was the multidimensional financial crisis which had hit in September 2008, wiping out the major investment banks, and creating a galloping recession that continued to shred jobs well into the first months of the Obama Presidency. The story of that crash has been told elsewhere, from every possible perspective, so there is no need to go over it in detail here. However, several moments are of particular importance to the Obama Presidency.

The first of these was then Senator Barack Obama's commitment to supporting the mass financial institutions bailout, the TARP, or Troubled Assets Recovery Program Bill, when the issue came to the vote in October 2008. It had been Obama's response to the crisis, and to the Bush administration's effort to find a bipartisan solution to it, that had allowed him to take the decisive lead in the election race, and guaranteed victory. In the weeks prior, John McCain had begun to level and then edge ahead, with a series of savvy political judo moves, to which the Democrats appeared to be incapable of responding effectively. The selection of Sarah Palin as a running mate had started to prove a negative, but it was McCain's disastrous response to the financial crisis, which occurred five days before the first of several scheduled debates between the candidates that proved crucial. While McCain announced that he was suspending his campaign and returning to Washington for the good of the country, Barack Obama took the unprecedented step of withdrawing to consult with advisors for two days before offering a response. McCain had always said that his style had been borne of his days as a fighter pilot, where split-second reaction was essential (even for such a disastrous practitioner of the profession as McCain). He took pride in being all tactics, no strategy. Obama's action was unprecedented, and risked the charge of being indecisive.

But by late September the American public was so frightened of the possible consequences of the crash, and so aware that it was moving out of the category of mere reversal, that the idea of action taken after considered reflection suddenly took on a whole new appeal. Overwhelmingly, the appeal of both John McCain and Sarah Palin had been on the basis of identity, not image – they were the sort of people many Americans rather imagined they wanted to be, the war hero and his sassy sidekick. But with the entire banking system sailing close to failure, the public rediscovered an older reason for political choice – elect the smartest guy in the room, precisely because he is not like you, ie bewildered. Obama's judicious handling of the crisis certified his claim to the Presidency, especially when he continued it into his own Presidency and extended its reach.

Though the TARP bill was for the most part a series of loans that were smartly repaid by the banks, this distinction never registered with the public, and neither the President nor other Democrats made any substantial effort to remind them of the fact. For many in the general public, this remained an enormous grant to the banks.

This was bad enough, but it was rendered worse by the Obama administration's simultaneous move, that of hiring as its crisis economic team a group of people from the same world and mindset that appeared to have made the crisis possible in the first place. It was not merely that one or two of the likes of Larry Summers, Timothy Geithner, and the like were being drawn back in from the world of Harvard and Goldman Sachs to create a plan; it was that all of them were, and no one but them. There was a total absence of more radical, progressive or dissident voices, those who, while possessing expertise, would come from areas other than the world of high finance.

The dismay that this produced in many who had supported or merely voted for Obama in 2008 after sitting out previous elections appears comprehensive and damaging, as is the degree to which it blindsided those who had been gearing up to go out and sell whatever compromises were necessary on healthcare, the freedom to organise (via limits to employer interference in union recognition balloting). 'Like a punch in the gut' was how one activist described it to me, a seemingly gratuitous turn back to the establishment, and a dispensing with the services of the activist base.

But if Obama's activist base had been spurned and to a degree dissolved, a base of a different type had started to form before the last (recorded) note of Yo Yo Ma's cello had faded on Inauguration Day. Though progressive critics would later pinpoint the birth of the Tea Party movement as occurring within a mass media context, a number of groups separate to both the Republican Party and the panoply of thinktanks and front groups surrounding it had already begun to form. Some of them arose from the political insurgency movement that had grown up around the Ron Paul, the radical libertarian Texas congressman and primary contender. Simultaneously a GOP congressman and Presidential candidate for the Libertarian Party, Paul had never made much secret of the fact that he regarded the Republican as a host body for his politics, and only mildly less uncongenial than the alternative. Earlier runs had created no great groundswell, but the perceived dismal failure of the Bush administration had caused such desperation among many that a space had been carved out into which Paul's movement could grow. Unkindly dubbed the 'Paultards' by some, they were a mixed bunch to say the least. Some saw themselves as libertarians, first and foremost, advocating a strictly minimal state; others were constitutionalists – fidelists really, believing themselves to be guardians of the pure spirit of the revolution, as set down in the Constitution. There were 'Tory anarchists', paleoconservatives who saw the neoconservative movement as an imperialist liberalism and a betrayal of all that conservatism stood for, and there were a small number from the anti-war left who had crossed over via the libertarian tradition. To varying degrees there were also racists, anti-semites, and 'truthers', those who believed that vast conspiracies could be unlocked by revealing the alleged fabrication of the 9.11 attacks.

The more positive elements of the Paul movement brought a tremendous energy to their cause, and some of the aleatoric performance art techniques last used by the left in the era of the yippies. They dubbed their movement the R(LOVE)ution, reversing the word within the word, a pure Woodstock gesture. They adopted black and orange as colours, and developed small motorised dirigibles to fly over the meetings of rival primary candidates. They set up tables outside too, and sometimes crossed the line from provocation to harassment. And when the Republicans came to St Paul Minnesota to coronate John McCain, they set up an alternative convention in the twin city of Minneapolis and called it Paulapalooza.

For decades there has been a strange hinterland at the right-wing edges of the Republican party, where people move between libertarian groups, constitutionalist groups and the mainstream party itself. But they've never had much ability to impose their will on the core of the Republican leadership, and contented themselves with being a permanent internal opposition. That power imbalance began to shift with the rise of the internet, social networking and Twitter, which removed some of the advantage of party leadership – its greater access to organisational technology. With the 2006 Congressional collapse and the 2008 Presidential loss, these groups gained their second advantage – the utter discrediting of mainstream Republicanism, and the demoralisation of its core operatives.

By 2009, some chapters within the 'Students for Ron Paul' had reformalised their organisation as 'Young Americans For Liberty', with the New York chapter staging a 'Tea Party' to protest against a range of specific tax rises by Democratic governor David Paterson. Keli Carender, a right-wing blogger in Seattle, organised a scratch 'Porkulus' protest in February 2009, just before the stimulus bill was signed into law. These protests already had the carnivale style that would become a Tea Party leitmotif, and one quite alien to Republican politics prior to the rise of the Paul movement. This was occurring at a time when the public face of the Republican party was Michael Steele, a hapless and slightly goofy organisation man, whose status as the first African-American head of the party was undercut by the suspicion that he only got it because no one else would take it.

Dirigibles and tricorn hats are alright, but it is unlikely that the proto-Tea Party would have got much further than oppositionality had a further group of people not been called to action by core media and then buttressed by very traditional and mainstream money. On February 19, CNBC cable channel commentator Rick Santelli made what even his supporters call a 'rant' from the floor of the Chicago Mercantile Exchange, attacking the (pretty meagre) provisions within both TARP and the stimulus package that would give some protection to foreclosed-upon mortgagees. Branding potential recipients 'losers' who were having their bad mortgages subsidised, Santelli received cheers from the surrounding traders. He urged those around to dump the government-backed derivatives in the river on July 1. The video was reproduced on the Drudge Report, and ceaselessly recycled on the right-wing cable media. Santelli had publicised a useful motif and a number of (pre-registered) websites sprung into action. Nationwide Tea Party protests were established, and then effectively publicised and supported by Fox News Channel, and a movement was born.

At what point the money came into this movement will always be a matter of debate. Some say it was always there, and the 'plain folks' being summoned to political activism by outrage were conservative organisers sent out under deep cover months before the movement began. At the very least the money was present at the near-beginning, with insider groups such as Dick Armey's FreedomWorks, Americans For Prosperity and several others rushing in to provide funding, training, equipment and support. Many of those who had felt called to the movement through the dark glass of Fox had always been Republicans, and whatever pluralist or outrider origins the movement might have had, by mid-2009 it was a solid Republican insurgency. As the parade headed down Main Street, two major figures scrambled to get in front of it: Fox TV personality Glenn Beck, and culture icon Sarah Palin.

Palin was by now known to the world, and possibly overexposed. Glenn Beck was in every sense a revelation. A mugging, primping, preening, whey-faced professional presenter, Beck had the air of a soapbox anti-fluoridation fanatic and the eyes of the late Marty Feldman. He'd started as a stand-up comedian, subsequently becoming a radio host and an alcoholic and multiple drug addictee. His recovery was achieved partly by converting to Mormonism, and pouring the energy of addiction into prophetic political apocalypticism.

Until 2008, he had been a presenter on CNN, part of their attempt to hold on to some of the right-wing audience drifting to Fox News. His show there had been a festival of feigned bemusement and incomprehension at a liberal secular-humanist 'culture of death', running on immoral debt. When he moved to FOX News he became a latter day Brigham Young, leading his followers out of the valley of death. His network more or less fused the Tea Parties into a national movement, and he added to it his '9.12' campaign – enumerating 12 virtues that had allegedly appeared the days after the World Trade Centre attacks.

Twelve virtues, gold plates handed down by angels...everything Beck did was perfused with the prophetic Americanism of the Mormon cult, which gave his performance an un-selfconscious drive that others could not imitate. Mormonism's origins as a revived white tribalism perhaps also influenced his statement that Barack Obama had a 'deep racist hatred of white people, a remark from the lower depths of the Tea Party's political traditions. He further teased around the limits of that politics by calling a march to 'Restore Honour' at the National Mall on the same day and place of Martin Luther King's 'March on Washington' day, forty-seven years earlier. His willingness to dissolve into tears because 'I love my country so much...and I fear we're losing it...' found a place in their hearts.

Sarah Palin, by contrast, touched them in a different way. Following a tumultuous vice-presidential campaign, the former sports journalist and Miss Congeniality Alaska had returned to her day job as governor of the state, and head of a rapidly growing cult. In mid-2009, she resigned the office, citing the deluge of ethics inquiries being directed at her in the state. Others suspected that the move had more to do with her burgeoning media career, and the fear that she might disappear from view a world away from the lower forty-eight. In 2009 her autobiography *Going Rogue* was released, to near frenzy; it would go on to sell two million copies. Her speaking fees were astronomical, her appearances frequent – many of them on FOX News for which she had become a commentator. She'd formed a PAC (a political action committee, a vehicle for drawing in donations), and had started to endorse potential Tea Party candidates and figures. Somewhere along the way, she'd picked up not only speed, but also polish and talent. Her resignation speech from the governorship had been rambling and free associative in the same manner as many of her 2008 campaign contributions. A year later, she – and many expert teachers – had refashioned that folksiness into a tighter and more compelling style. She'd also succeeded in internalising a consistent philosophy of sorts, the supercharged fuel of laissez-faire economics and American exceptionalism that much of the Tea Party was running on.

By the second quarter of 2010 it was clear to all that any fantasies the Republican Party might have had of controlling her were in vain. Propped up by the ever-reliable FOX, she not only joined with the insurgent force of the Tea Party, she began shaping a newly branded type of activist, the 'mama grizzlies' – right-wing women, spruiking a conservative message that nevertheless eschewed many of the traditional gender roles that earlier female conservatives had advanced. This was a smart and successful move, because many of these women had an energy that their men lacked. Doubtless this too had been thrashed out by an expert consultant team – '"eagle mamas!" no, "lady killers", um...' – but it also tapped into a real phenomenon, and one that left many on the left looking tired and beaten down.

Throughout all this time, the Obama administration and the Pelosi-led Democratic majority in the House had been relentlessly putting up new bills, trying to roll through one of the most quantitatively ambitious programmes of recent memory. In mid-2009, the Democrats had briefly gained a nominal filibuster-proof majority in the Senate, after Wisconsin's Al Franken had been finally seated, and Pennsylvania's Arlen Specter had transferred to the Democrats after thirty years as a Republican. After a year-long fight, a reconciled health care bill was passed at the end of March 2010. Acts passed in the lead-up to that had included the American Recovery and Reinvestment Act, a Fair Pay act, a mortgage default relief act, control of credit card conditions, and several more.

Alas, for want of a nail. The death of Edward Kennedy in August 2009 occasioned a special election in Massachusetts, at a time when multiple, and contradictorily motivated, dissatisfaction was at an all-time high. The Massachusetts Democrats put up an uninspiring organisation woman as candidate with more than an air of entitlement to the seat. The Republicans chose Scott Brown, a former male centrefold who drove a truck. A poll showed that sixty per cent of voters wanted the new senator to continue Ted Kennedy's work; sixty per cent of them also wanted her or him to oppose Obama's health care plan. Since Edward Kennedy's great cause had been a health care plan considerably to the left of Obama's proposal, this was an early sign that the American public was suffering from advancing cognitive dissonance. Massachusetts was the archetypally liberal state; nevertheless it selected Brown to represent it in the Senate, and with the endorsement of Sarah Palin. He would prove to be somewhat more pragmatic than his out-of-state backers had imagined, but he was the means by which the Democrats fell beneath the number required for 'cloture' – the sixty votes required to end a filibuster.

Throughout 2010, more than 375 bills passed in the House and filibustered in the Senate would mount into the hundreds. They included the Paycheck Fairness Act, the Wounded Veteran Job Security Act, the Free Flow of Information Act, the Vision Care For Kids Act, and many more. That wasn't the only thing mounting up for President Obama and the Democrats. By September 2010, the unemployment rate was still at 9.6%, having barely budged from its high in early 2009. The $800 billion stimulus package was having little visible economic fact – and even less of a political one, the Democrats inexplicably not claiming credit for the tax breaks they had extended to tens of millions of people, or much more besides. Even the very first provisions of the new healthcare bill would not kick in until a few weeks before the election, and most were not due to come on line until 2014, by which time they may well have been repealed.

Smaller and more particular crises had sprung up and been handled badly – Obama had passed remarks on the arrest of prominent black professor Henry Louis Gates, who had been handcuffed by a white policeman, in his own home, the event which had provoked Beck's accusation of a hatred of white people. Obama's remark that the arrest was 'stupid' was the perfectly worst intervention in the matter – neither rising above it by refusing to weigh in from executive power on a police matter, nor coming in strongly about the racism that sees even a distinguished man treated like a punk. Faced with a backlash, he was obliged to conduct an embarrassing 'beer summit' between Gates, the police officer and poor old Joe Biden, in an attempt to blunt the damage.

It was a mistake he would repeat in the matter of the 'Ground Zero mosque' – the non-mosque not on Ground Zero that was attracting vociferous attack as a 'victory mosque' planted on a field of blood. Obama initially gave some succour to raddled liberals by appealing to the notion of freedom of religion as a founding principle of the Republic – only to walk it back twenty-four hours later with the remark that he wasn't applying it to any particular case, a legalistic formulae near-perfectly designed to piss off absolutely everyone. In between there was the BP spill, which the White House took a gamble on, hoping it would be resolved before they were called on to own it – thus ensuring that it became theirs only when the problem had become intractable. Issue after issue, Obama couldn't take a win, not despite the hedging of political bets, but because of it.

None of this had improved by the time the primary season for the midterms came round, and the Tea Party had the smell of blood in their nostrils. They, and the right-wing establishment of the Republican party that had grafted itself into their nucleus, were further emboldened by a landmark decision of the Supreme Court –

Citizens United vs FCC, delivered in January 2010, which struck down key provisions of the McCain-Feingold limits on political spending that did not go directly to candidates. *Citizens United* re-opened the briefly closed floodgates, making huge attack campaigns possible, turning the focus of both primaries and the midterms themselves to that of vicious takedown.

The Tea Party would later say that it had elevated more than a hundred candidates in the Republican primary battles. This is nonsense, of course. The majority of those endorsed by Tea Party groups – by mid-2010 there were six major Tea Party peak bodies – were right-wing Republicans who were likely or certain to get their party's nomination in any case. In other places, Tea Party-supported candidates displaced establishment candidates, and sometimes incumbents. The threat from the right had already pushed Arlen Specter to take the Democratic whip as a desperate survival strategy in Pennsylvania. Now they despatched Senate candidate presumptive, Governor Charlie Crist in Florida, replacing him with second-generation Cuban exile Marco Rubio who made a passion of American exceptionalism; Ken Buck in Colorado. In Alaska, Joe Miller bested the incumbent Lisa Murkowski (with a lot of help from the Palins, who were engaged in a two-decade war with the Murkowski dynasty). In Nevada, Sharron Angle was put up against Senate majority leader Harry Reid, a man with a vast network of supporters to draw on, and state achievements to point to. Most spectacularly, the Republican party of Delaware selected perpetual candidate Christine O'Donnell over the state's Republican congressman-at-large Mike Castle, who had been a shoo-in to win the special election to fill the seat vacated by Joe Biden.

As October came round, and the campaign proper swung into gear, the Democrats were polling behind by around seven to eight per cent. Some numbers were looking up for them. Though unemployment remained high, new jobs were beginning to be created month-on-month. The first changes made by the healthcare act – the extension of Medicaid to new categories of people, a ban on insurance companies denying coverage to people with pre-existing conditions –

were beginning to kick in. Could the President sell the American people on the idea of a journey only begun, a hard road turning upwards? Could he turn out his base and mitigate the losses? As the campaign went into the final fortnight, the Democrats were still running an average of 6% behind. Some major stroke of genius or luck would be required to minimise the losses. To even it out, they would need something spectacular. But the energy was all with the Right. Delaware seemed to be a great place to start...

2.

Tea Partying in Delaware with the White Witch

Blue skies over the town, with a trace of cloud moving fast across the sky. At the edge of a large field, away from the Home Depot and Arby's on North Dupont highway, there's the Delaware agricultural museum, housed in a copy of a traditional red barn. Nine times the size of the real thing, it makes itself strange, like a Claes Oldenburg. To one side, there's a mini-colonial village, three or four reconstructed houses and a general store. Out the front Steve, a beefy guy, whose every item of clothing, from baseball cap to belt, advertises a major agricultural manufacturer, is setting up a small pavilion tent at the car park entrance. 'Spending Revolt.com' is on its side as he fits the poles together. Folks are already arriving. Everyone knows everyone else.

'Gonna be a big one Steve?' someone asks, passing through.

'Naw,' he says, a little downcast, 'it's too windy.'

Welcome to the Tea Party, Delaware-style. Although this isn't an official Tea Party event. It's a stop on the road of the 'Spending Revolt' bus, yet another of the hundreds of organisations that have sprung up, after some pretty extensive irrigation, over the last eighteen months – and particularly since the January Citizens United supreme court ruling. The bus, a red white and blue behemoth, covered in graffiti garnered at each stop on its nationwide progress from California ('who is John Galt?' 'take our country back'), sits outside the museum, forming the backdrop to a makeshift stage. The car park is filling up with people, farming types and military retirees, attached to the nearby air force base. About eighty all told, mostly senior citizens, all white – comfortable, sprawling in cheap shirts and slacks, they're on the way to being outnumbered by the foreign press. Around twenty young people in dark suits and jackets, all mistaking each other for the tour organisers. At the side of the podium there's a three or four sharp local types – well-dressed men, and two women in tan and beige, faux leopard print scarves holding their hair in, saucer-size shades hiding the crow's feet.

The music cranks up as the crowd swells towards low triple figures, 'Don't Stop Believin', 'Walking on Sunshine', ancient pop-rock that's become the house music for these events. The harassed press officer, fending off queries from *Le Monde* and *Asahi Shimbun* as to whether Christine O'Donnell will be appearing, nods to a large woman, who responds in a deep southern accent.

'We gonna start this?'

'Let's start this.'

'Ladies and gentlemen,' she says, 'I'm Amy for Americans for Prosperity and welcome to the revolution!'

There's a cheer.

'Now I'd like to introduce Ted Turner—'

There's confusion.

'No, it's Jim Martin from Sixty Plus.'

A lean moustachioed man gets up, 'a veteran' (cheers), to announce that he ain't Ted Turner, he's from Sixty Plus, the insurgent retirees organisation, 'we aint the AARP, which is now a multi-billion dollar insurance combine, an organisation which made Harry Belafonte their man of the year, a supporter of Ugo Chavez'. Boos, but then John notices the press scribbling furiously, and thinks quick. 'Not that Harry ain't a great entertainer, but our patron is Pat Boone, who has five children and I dunno how many grandchildren!'. Cheers.
John sets out the argument 'we're takin' our country back, we've had enough of being taxed by an unrepresentative government', but we're all only waiting for one thing.

'I know you're only waiting for one person, and here she is, the next Senator from Delaware, Christine O'Donnell!'

There's a flash of blue and here she is on stage, the Republican candidate from one of the smallest states in the union, suddenly world famous, a sign of the Tea Party rising, a certified Palin Mama Grizzly, a Biblical literalist, and a former part-time witch.

'How y'all doing Delaware?'

There's a cheer. She's their gal. She's their gal because Sarah has anointed her. Because she is Sarah now, more or less. She was always like her. Now the likeness is both deliberate and uncanny, the mannish suit, the chestnut hair, dyed to look natural.

'We're going to take our country back!'

There it is again, that notion that not merely power, but their whole national being has been taken from them. She launches into her opponent Chris Coons, a central-casting liberal, mild-mannered and lacking in vim. 'He's raised taxes 54%, he almost sent New Castle county broke, like all Democrats he spells taxes F.E.E.!' that gets a huge laugh. She launches into the estate tax – ie death duties – which, for obvious reasons, the TP is playing up.

'Yesterday I heard a sad story...about a sick old man who is literally praying to die before January 1, so that he'll be able to pass on the money he earned before the IRS "redistributes" it. Well send me to Washington and that won't happen. We're behind in the polls, but we're catching up, so keep fighting keep doing it and we'll get there'.

Enormous cheers, and already with a touch of the regal Palin air she sweeps off the stage,surrounded by professional political types who'd been hiding from the cameras behind the stand. Barrelling through the press, they enter the barn through a side entrance. There's other speakers, the official Tea Party rep – 'if we don't prevail in 2010, there won't be a 2012', and Glen Urquhart, the Reps candidate (Delaware is a sole district), who is famous for claiming that the separation of church and state was invented by Adolf Hitler. But the mood went with Christine and a few people drift off.

The press are all at the back, vox popping either the most hickish-looking types they can find, or the tan-clad leopardines, Republican silvertails, one of the half-dozen families that have run Delaware since it was a plantation on the river. I look for someone who might give an informed view from the inside, but he finds me first – Dan, a stocky redhead, cheap-dressed too, but indoor gamer, not back-of-a-tractor style. Freckled and soft-spoken, he has the demeanour of a man who had spent a lot of time reading Robert Nozick with the drapes drawn against the sun. Behind us Tea Party lady, Donna, has set up a call-and-return: 'That's not government! That's...' 'TYRANNY!' the crowd yells back.

'Here's what I'm interested in —'

'You wanna know about the Tea Party?'

His hand was in my hand, shaking it, even before I spoke. It was a couple of seconds before I realised it had his card in it.

'Here's what I don't understand,' I continued. 'The original Tea Party was a revolt against dictatorial authority —'

'Well it was a revolt against tax —'

'Yeah, but it was a revolt against unrepresentative imposition of tax. You're opposing an administration you don't like that's headed by the 44th representative of the system put in its place. How is it tyranny?'

'Well it's more that it's unrepresentative. Congress has accrued to itself powers that aren't in the Constitution and they are passing unconstitutional laws. The health care bill is an unconstitutional law...'

'Yeah, but that's what the Supreme Court is for...'

'Mmmmm,' said Ron, 'but the Supreme Court, indeed all the courts, have become too liberalised —'

'OK, but even if I agreed with that, that's simply part of the process of selection and confirmation —'

'Yes but some of these justice should have been impeached. That's what the founders intended. But Congress won't do it.'

'Why not?'

'That's the question,' said Ron. 'That's why we want different Congressmen. Ysee it's all the fault of the Senate. The 17th amendment is when we really departed from the Founders' intent. The states should select Senators to represent them, they shouldn't be directly elected.'

'Yeah but no one gets up and talks about the direct election of Senators. They talk about tax, as if it were tyrannically imposed...'

'Well it is because the Senate...'

Round and round it went for half an hour. I should have been spending time trying to find a birther who would talk about fluoridation, but Ron was giving me what you rarely get in the media, the rational version, agree with it or not, of the Tea Party's case.

On stage the official Tea Party rep was losing the crowd, telling them how the FDA was ruining her health food business by capricious inspection of goods, 'and this has been going on since they used 9.11 to put in all sorts of laws we don't need'. Nine-eleven? Pretext? Unnecessary laws? The crowd didn't like that. They were silent, down-mouthed. Dover base is where the troops come home through, the living and the dead, flag-draped coffins coming out of cargo holds in the early-morning dark. It's not a place to air sentiments anti-military, however attenuated. Jennifer looked on, concerned. When Donna launched back into a more fruitful vein – 'I'm not going to be taxed out of existence', Amy piped up. 'I'm not either, how bout you?' 'NO WAY!' the crowd roared back.

Ron had finished laying out his argument – that national power equals bureaucracy, bureaucracy is by definition unrepresentative if derived from unconstitutional power.

'So it is tyrannous?'

He glanced over at the old homesteads. 'Yes, I think I would say tyrannous.'

They'd ended with Jim Martin announcing that Christine O'Donnell had been chosen for an award by...Pat Boone! It was bizarre, the emphasis on Boone who made his career rerecording black hits for white audiences, having judiciously removed all the rhythm. He is of ancient vintage, even for this crowd. It was a nostalgia for prior nostalgia. French TV was interviewing the tan ladies before an enormous American flag, as people signed the bus. 'We're not going to take it!' Twisted Sister announced from the PA.

Back at the motel, I could hear drumming from the campus of Delaware State U across the lake. It was homecoming weekend, when American students return to college and high school, and huge celebrations occur, a parade in the morning, a game in the afternoon, partying, shots, and sex on neat lawns through the night. On TV, they're replaying the Nevada Senate candidates' debate between Tea Partier Sharron Angle, and majority leader, the seemingly hapless Harry Reid. The debate is one that Angle is widely held to have won, projecting passionate anger at the apparent blitheness and profligacy of the government of which Reid is a part. Nevada's economy, fuelled by a real-estate boom derived from mass population influx to service the tourism and gambling industries, has been hit harder than most, as millions of Americans decide that they've lost enough money in their daily lives, without needing to go to Vegas to lose the remainder of it.

Angle is short, with a brown bob haircut, and a red-painted mouth that looks like she's been razor-cut from ear-to-ear. She has a tremendous vengeful energy about her, and more than a touch of Madame Mao. Reid looks like a lamb you just hit with the side of your car, and whose neck you are now obliged to snap, from mercy. She flays him on government spending, and on the lack of jobs in Nevada, without being pinned down on how she would solve the latter, or cut to mitigate the former.

Reid, defending a terrible economic situation can only ask people to hold on, and appeal to bare desperation by trumpeting his insider status and how that will help Nevada to attract federal money. After one exchange, Reid was reduced to bleating 'she's extreme...she's extreme ' Towards the end, perhaps concerned that she hadn't landed a killer blow on the old sparrer, Angle accused Reid of corruption, wondering aloud how someone 'who came from Searchlight, Nevada' had subsequently done so well. 'Where did that money come from Harry Reid?' she said, continuing her tactic throughout, of referring to him by his full name. Reid responded that he'd done well as a lawyer, and subsequently invested successfully. The Angle campaign had tried this earlier, accusing him of living high on the hog in the Washington Ritz-Carlton, a standard four-star hotel in which Reid keeps what is effectively a one-bedroom serviced apartment.

Such manoeuvres are risky, and rely on an assumption of terrific backwardness among Nevadans – and may be testament to the visceral and personal hatred fuelling Angle's campaign. For no matter how much many Nevadans loathe Reid, and many do, no one would look at him and see a man-on-the-take – a judgement that is less a tribute to Reid than it is awareness that his one passion in life is the relentless accumulation of the sort of personal insider power that the US Senate runs on. His lifelong pursuit of this is the reason why this utterly unprepossessing man has become head of one chamber of the most powerful government in the world. But it has also made him utterly incapable of responding to the populist politics that Angle channels, the shrill cry of right and hurt she directs against the establishment. The resounding moment of this debate was when she told her male opponent to 'man up, Harry Reid', the remark that launched a thousand cultural studies dissertations.

Flick around, and it's Sarah Palin on TV, wowing them at a California rally. It's all Mama Grizzlies, all the time. In the signature red jacket, hair piled high, she powers out her message to near hysterical acclaim. The plastic frame of the TV buzzes with the static bursts of cheering.

'You know so great to be in the state that gave us the great Ronald Reagan yeahhh. See all the Mama Grizzlies out there you've been ridiculed, you've been mocked, you've been slandered by the left.' Cheering. 'Still you didn't let the big government-loving professional politicians and the complicit left-wing, lamestream media tell you to sit down and shut up. Instead no, you didn't retreat. You reloaded. And you've turned this country around.' Huge, sustained, cheering. Two years on, the know-nothingness has gone, filled out with some solid tuition in conservative libertarianism. 'We gotta get back to the American exceptionalism that Ronald Reagan talked about you know and once we restore our republic we restore our free markets, and you know well I can see 2012 from my house!' Her speeches are brilliantly written, her delivery electrifying, a sing-song jazzy rhythm, half Mama Grizzly, half mean girl, dripping with sarcasm and triumph. I have heard nothing like it, ever. This is all either one of the greatest shows of recent times, or the start of something very big.

Out the window, the sun was setting over the lake. Kids were pulling into the motel lot out front, taking rooms to party on in after the official ceremonies. The wind was still up, and the clouds were moving fast.

3.

Organising for Indiana: Rusted on in the Rust-Belt

'dugan', indiana
monday 18 october*

Outside the Casa Verde bar and grill, you can see the steam forming on the windows. It's eight in the evening, and the remainder of the street is deserted, though there's a coupla other bars, lit up at the other end. They look like pretty trad taverns, a Miller Lite neon sign in the window, the even bump of country music bass coming out the door. The Casa Verde has a bike rack out front and a sign saying 'chai!' in the window. There's a bin for the Indianapolis street press newspaper at the curb. It is at the centre, and appears to constitute the entirety, of the boho section of this mid-size Indiana town.

Inside, it's the usual arrangement, mismatched tables and chairs, more posters, a small board of laser-printed ads advertising band personnel and second-hand laptops, a few phone number tags torn off the bottom of them. There's a wall menu with sombrero kitsch surrounding it, though the contents are eclectic. A couple of people in the front, picking at burritos and bean salads. Down the back, there's a few tables pushed together with half a dozen people around them, and a buzz drifting up to the front: 'Hello I'm calling on behalf of Simon Sam...hello have you voted yet in the election...hello did you know the Republicans are poised to retake...'. They're all young but one, using their own phones to make the calls. There's an eight-socket powerboard at the centre of the table, with a few chargers plugged in. 'Hello...did you vote in the 2008 election...this is a more important election...hello hello hello...'

The Tea Party have the carnivale this year. Against them, the Democrats have Organising For America, their get-out-the-vote organisation, a nationwide roll-call of neighbourhood phone banks, canvassers, house parties to make phone calls, and street gatherings to kick off canvassing. There's not much partying here, of any kind – simply a grim effort to get out the vote that elected Barack Obama in 2008, and limit the gains of the Republicans to substantial, rather than catastrophic. Thousands of these take place all over the country, all listed on the Organising For America's website. You bring your own phone and charger, they give you a script if you want it, or some talking points if you think you can wing it. You either call your own friends, or work from a list, or both. It's double-duty – convince people that they should vote Democrat, and then make sure they actually get out and do it. Jen, a twenty-something liberal arts student – dark, unstyled hair, glasses, track top – is the organiser. She's optimistic about the result, thinks the party can hold off Republican control of the House, and that there's 'no chance' that the GOP will take the Senate. But her voice is strained, and she sounds tired.

'Sure midterms are always tough. The vote goes down. This time round there's a star factor missing. We're going to take some hits.'

'We're going to take all hits in Indiana,' says one of the other bankers. 'Hello – hey Dave, hey man, you gonna vote...'

'Well I don't think that's necessarily true, but yeah, the odds are against. Taking this state in oh eight was ... amazing. We hadn't won Indiana since sixty eight.'

'Hello, I'm calling on behalf of …'

'Hi, is that arrrrhhh Macy. Macy you expressed an interest in volunteering for...'

'So, are numbers down this time?'

'Numbers for what?' Jen is polite but at the edge of touchy.

'Well for everything – commitment to vote, numbers here.'

'Sure but I'm confident they'll pick up in the final week. We'll get the vote out.' I hadn't arranged this visit through the party – a near impossible process in any case – but they didn't need to worry about Jen. She had the script in her head.

She'd effectively organised this cell out of the college she attends. It's in the next town, a third-tier university, and a few of the students live in Dugan, making the place part-student, mostly agricultural. Four of the other five volunteers are students, kids in their early twenties, in the flyover slacker uniform, down-at-heel standard issue jeans and sweat tops, with the occasional touch of ironic hipster – a goatee with a vandyke moustache, a Blue Oyster cult t-shirt. The sixth person is Penny, a fifty-something woman with a perm and pharmacy-issue reading glasses. She has a slightly more querulous air to her patter, but she makes two calls to every one made by any of the others, ploughing down the list.

But they're all working hard, and without much of that hopey changey thing to run on. Having spent a year and some months failing to sell their achievements and/or scare the bajingo out of folks with horror tales of a Republican return, the Democratic campaign is a virtual nullity. Worse, the leadership has decided that the issue to campaign on is campaign funding, and the possibility that foreign money is mixed in with donations to the Republicans, or for attack ads in their favour. The focus is bizarre, bewildering, a perfect anti-campaign, courting charges of xenophobia without getting any sort of bang out of it.

'I'm not even using the foreign money script,' says Carrie, a pre-med (ie science student). 'I'm just telling people get out and vote motherfucker. I'm not even calling people in this district. This one's gone. We've got a chance northwards. I'm calling people there.' She's getting sharp looks from Jen. 'I better get back to this. Hello, is that Miles? Miles, I'm calling from...'

'For the record,' says Jen, 'though you're not using our names are you...? For the record, I don't think we should give up on any districts...'

'I do,' says the vandyke.

'I'm just calling the list,' says Penny. 'Just call the list.'

You wouldn't want to underestimate the cumulative power of such work: solid, unflashy, it may fight the Republican money-machine to a standstill by election day, limit the hurt. But by the same token, you can't help but feel the sense of inwardness to it, the ritual quality. Snug in the Casa Verde, with its posters for campus activities and Guided By Voices turned low on the speakers upfront, the street press on the table with its Ziggy comic and Dan Savage advice column, the OFA phonebank is just one of those things you do as a progressive student, a folk activity, a kind of quilting for the info era. The folks here are amazed when I tell them that this sort of campaigning doesn't happen in the same way, or at least in anything like the same volume.

All politics has a degree of ritual of course, and these people have simply answered the party call. But OFA phonebanks across the nation seem to be staffed by such people, young progressives, students on a type of UNESCO mission aimed inland. Where are the people they're calling? Why such a gap between the mobilisers and the mobilised?

'I can't really give you a good answer for that,' says Penny, when I manage to tear her away from her phone for a few minutes. 'See everyone in my family is a Republican. Even my husband's a Republican. But I've always, I dunno, I've always thought we gotta help people.' It's never been difficult to avoid politics among the people she lives with, she says, but since 2007, 'it's become harder.' More than that she will not say.

'Hell, it's so long since this state was really Democratic. I mean it is up north, Gary and all that, but not down here. I can't see it ever being Democrat down here again.'

'We really need to get back to work,' Jen says, no-nonsense. Then, in horror of sounding rude, 'of course, this is a cafe and you're welcome to stay. But,' she looks over at the serving counter, 'I think they'll want you to order a coffee or some chai or something.'

*personal names and that of the town have been changed.

4.

Hello, Goodbye, Columbus

the republican road trip hits ohio,
tuesday 19 october

someday we shall return...goodbye Columbus, goodbye Columbus...

Whatever else it may be, Columbus, Ohio is a city that punches above its weight. It's the headquarters of Nationwide Insurance, Limited Brands Inc, and Big Lots Inc, among others, and the place where the first Wendy's opened, and the site, now a vacant lot in a streetcorner park, has a cast-iron commemorative sign of a size which gives it a historical weighting more or less equal to the Battle of Kursk. At the edge of its downtown stands Ohio State University, an educational behemoth, whose enormous medical school hospital complex has eaten up whole neighbourhoods, and whose vast stadia could easily accommodate a small-to-moderate size Olympics. Its city blocks are enormous, and its plethora of 60s and 70s international-style skyscrapers have a *Mad Men* nostalgia feel to them, row after row after Mies van Der Rohe, the sort of places where you could get a steak dinner at the Red Room, and pay with a cardboard Diners Club card.

Beyond that, and its well preserved and restored civic and religious buildings, it has been substantially planed flat. Vast car parks stretch between the squared-off streets, where all the small stuff once was, all the little buildings, all the scumble. Glass curtain walls sparkle over vast vacancies, and the effect is now without its appeal, a

Forbidden City that has escaped the greater damage done to Ohio as a whole, a state that was, until recently, little more than a vast auto-parts workshop. It is awful, in the archaic sense of the term, leaning on the awe, and the scattered folks on the street – those who don't use the skyways, connecting building to building – seem diminished by it.

So it was probably wise for the Fire Pelosi! Bus to make its southern Ohio pitstop a little out of town, at the Better Business Bureau Business Park, a beige single-storey office strip mall near the bend in the river, host to the Ohio Grocers Association, a discount medical imaging centre and the Columbus Republican Victory Office. There were forty or so faithful on hand in the car park for the arrival of the bright orange tourliner, and not much Tea Partyesque bonhomie in evidence. This tour was being helmed by Michael Steele, the reasonable, intelligent, disastrous African-American head of the Republican National Committee, and the turn-out was Republican mainstreamers, young men in mid-priced jackets and chinos, young Republican co-eds given a t-shirt, told to look pretty and possibly fingerbanged afterwards, and a couple of old geezers taking the elders' licence to dress wacky, the gals in stars and stripes earrings, men with flag pants and ear-hair.

Everyone knew each other, greeted each other as they drove into the carpark. No Tea Party style here. TP events have an entirely different feel, unruly, slightly raffish, somewhere between a country fair and a medieval peasants crusade in which everyone has made their own armour out of barrels, a carnivale of loners, netizens and militias drawn momentarily together from the vast American matrix. This crowd had all been at last night's Shriners Tombola at the Hampton Inn ballroom. The smallest Tea Party event can get in reporters from all over the world. The Fire Pelosi Bus was attended by the Columbus Dispatch, the local CBS affiliate, and one Australian journalist desperate for a story.

'Can we have a little noise?' said the cameraman to the co-ed cheer squad, as the flame orange bus appeared at the turn into the car park, and sailed straight past. Then it appeared again, coming backwards, slowly, and backing into the park. It took eight minutes.

The co-eds kept cheering, then realised they would have to stop and re-start. Everyone else just waited, signs held at their hips. No one knew where to look.

As far as Steele goes, that phenomenon is not exclusive to Columbus. The Fire Pelosi bus is apparently all his own idea, a barely staffed ghost campaign wandering the country, that party critics charge to be of little effect – and overwhelmingly oriented to Michael Steele's quest for a second term as RNC chair. Two years after their disastrous loss across the board, the Republican party still hasn't really got its act together, and the Fire Pelosi bus is a symptom of that – old-skool party rules barrelling down the highway.

Had they been going into this election solo, their chances of regaining the House would be slim indeed, but Fox News, the Tea Party, and, let's face it, the Democrats have saved their asses. Even the Pelosi bus, with its appearance of partyless agitprop, is a steal from the Teaheads. The fact they've had to back it in slowly to the Grocers Association parking space is, in that respect and as we say, far from coincidental. This is what the Republican Party and campaign would look like had it not been taken to a new level and new places, by a network of political professionals buttressing some enthusiastic amateurs. These are the folks from the country club nineteenth-hole bar. They're the people the advertisers aim at now, which is why you never see a soft drink or CD ad on TV, only wall-to-wall publicity for car insurance and Cialis ('see our ad in Golf Magazine'). They are the 'forties wave boomers in their pelf. Though they were under twenty-five at the time of Woodstock, it is impossible to imagine them ever being young.

'Heya heya, what is up Columbus!'. Steele's emerged from the doors, rallying the troops, trying to sell a little bit of style. Tall and gangly, bald and neatly moustachioed, he's always seemed like a basically nice guy, gently spoken and never vicious, maybe a little awkward. For that reason the *Daily Show* represents him with a purplish muppet, whom Jon Stewart occasionally interviews about the state of the GOP.

That's a little bit racist, but watching him, in a suburban parking-lot glad-handing the crowd it's difficult not to think that among the number of people who should never try to act black can be counted Michael Steele. He's the Vanilla Ice of Republican politics.

'We're here to thank you! You know the Democrats were bragging to me that they'd made four hundred thousand calls a few weeks ago. And I could tell them we'd made eight million!' Moderate cheering. 'How bout dat!'. Cheering withers. 'Thank you thank you. Thank you for extracting us from the jumble of politics that we had lost ourselves in after November 2008.' A little booing. 'It goes without saying that Ohio is a very important state this and every year...' Goes without saying it do. Outside of the glass towers of Columbus, Ohio has been hit hard by a double wave – for years the continued decline of the auto industry has seen the state lose good union jobs that had been held for two and sometimes three generations. The '08 crisis came on top of that, destroying many of the less secure jobs that auto workers had drifted to. Other places have been hit harder, but Ohio had been the centre of a well-paid, secure working class, and the shift – the shift backwards – has left the state reeling.

Having voted for the Democrats in 08, Ohio is now swinging back into the red zone, with the Democrats facing a loss of as many of four House seats in a state of 18 districts, the election of a Republican senator to an open seat, and a neck-and-neck race for the position of governor, currently occupied by Democrat Ted Strickland. These all matter, but the governorship matters more than most places, because the road to Republican victory in 2012 passes through the buckeye state. For all the Republicans' bluster, regaining the White House will be a tougher proposition than regaining the House no matter how much corporate money is shovelled in. That's not only because Obama remains a charismatic leader who can be a great campaigner on seven of every twenty days, but also because they have to win everything back and then some. The Democrats can lose Ohio – and Florida and Indiana, or any two or three other states – and still scrape back in. Barring strange and terrible events, the GOP has to get Ohio. In 2004 they won the state, in an election many believe was at best dirty, at worst stolen. Should the 2012 election turn on a few thousand votes, control of the statehouse may make all the difference as to what gets counted and how. Steele knows this, and there are signs of more than usual life – well, life – in his stump speech. 'We have got to get this state back to work.' More cheering. Actually, Ohio is getting back to work. By the time the wave of the recession peaked in 2009, unemployment in the state was 16% in major urban areas. When you add in the underemployment and involuntary retirement that that covers, you would be heading for 30%. That's a depression. By September this year it was back down to 12%, and heading south. President Obama was here a few days, to speak in one of the larger stadia. He spoke of slow progress, of foreign money, of difficult days ahead, of the Republicans wanting back the car they drove into the ditch, to drive it back in again. But he never thumped the lectern and said 'damn it, they gave you a depression. A depression. We're getting out of it together. Don't stop now. They'll put you right back in one. You're not stupid Ohio. Don't act stupid.'

Shoulda said it, never did. Now a poll shows that independent voters in Ohio want three things: to sack the Democrats, reduce the deficit, and commence massive job creation schemes. There's a lot of it about. Last night's Senate race debate in West Virginia saw the Democratic candidate Joe Manshin trying every trick in the book to avoid getting blindsided by the Republican contender John Raese. Manshin is a popular governor doing his best for a state which is another contender in the vote-against-your-own-interests Olympics. Whole mountain-tops are lopped off by the mining industry, who give back not much more than average-paid jobs and a pollution bill to be picked up by the state. Those who benefit live nowhere near the giant quarry the state has become. They include John Raese, who lives in Florida, and inherited his nine-figure fortune, something he said he wanted 'to give all Americans the chance to do.' You have to admire that insouciance, that sort of political dada-panache. Only in a polity where progressives have allowed myths to circulate unchallenged and uncontested can a blazered CEO with a halo of fluffed white hair and a South Beach tan claim inheritance of wealth and power as the fulfilment of the American dream. He should be on a Bolshevik-style poster, being swept away by Lenin – who could have got a good 20% in this state in the 1920s. Instead Raese is on the ballot, and leading by two points. There's no polite way to say it: the once savvy American industrial working class is utterly addled, and that is what permits the shadow party of the Republicans to claim that they represent the general will, as Michael Steele is doing here.

'Try and imagine what headline you'd like to see on November 3 in the *Columbus Dispatch* – it is the Dispatch isn't it?' he says to a very little laughter. The fat old Dispatch roundsman scribbling in a pad looked dreamy at that ('Dispatch to survive another three years' perhaps). 'What would you like to see?'

'You're fired!' someone yells. Everyone laughs big at that one, Steele a little less easily, suspecting it's not Pelosi that one's directed at. 'Well Columbus, make it happen!'.

Big cheer, and then the crowd starts to disperse. Whoever's going to make it happen, it's not going to be these folks. There's a couple of kids in blue blazers, tan chinos, and white open neck shirt. Young Republican standard-issue leisurewear. Scuba-diving, they would fall backward off the boat, masked, tanked, and in a blue blazer, tan chinos with a white open-neck shirt.

'Hi, do you want to sign the petition?'. A young, thin woman in jeans and a windbreaker has been sharking around the crowd with a clipboard and pen. I'd noticed her before. She doesn't look like your average GOPer, and the other staffers didn't seem to have much to do with her.

'What's it for?'

'It's to get a state constitutional amendment on the ballot for next time banning Obamacare.'

'OK,' I said. 'Here's one question I have, that a lot of foreigners watching this election have – a lot of people object to the Obama healthcare plan because it's socialist, but they seem to defend Medicare. But as far as we can see Medicare's simply a public health programme with an age-limit. How does that square off?' She seemed a reasonable type to ask about this.

She wasn't.

'You can't call Medicare a socialist programme! They're taking from Medicare, and turning it into a rationed system! It's not like the NHS where people get told to die!'

'O..K...' I said, steadying myself a little, 'but rationing isn't the essence of whether a system is socialist or not. I mean Europe and Australia have public systems where there's no rationing. And Medicare you pay a tax in, you get care out later, regardless of what you paid in. Isn't that socialised health care in essence?'

'But it's not rationed! We have the best healthcare system in the world!'

'But you plainly don't. You pay double everyone else and you die at the same age – actually two years younger, but that's because of the extra homicide rate. And forty million people have no insurance.'

'But they can always go to an emergency room!'

'But —'

'You can't say we're not generous. This is the most generous country in the world.'

'Well I didn't, but it isn't...'

'Why does everyone want to come here?'

'Because you share a border with the third world! Two million people try and get into Greece and the EU for the same reason! You think it's because they like the zorba dance?'

'Look well you have your opinions,' she said, 'and everytime I give mine, you disagree with me.' She stormed off.

You disagree with me. The horror, the horror. If I had got the rational and constitutional case for the Republican insurgency in Delaware, this was its other, anti-Obamaism cut from whole cloth. It was a series of memes and talking points, barely alighted on before moving to the next, rationing, socialism, best in the world, most generous nation, everyone wants to come here, rationing around and around. It is incantatory for the base, but it's meant to be. That's what a base is for. The signal fact of the 2010 election is how spellbinding it has become for ever-wider and more traumatised sections of the wider American public.

There's time for photos after that, and the assembled Republican candidates – all very white, save for one Asian woman running for a state assembly seat – start to disperse pretty quickly.

The state chairman, a John Raese lookalike, was inserting himself into his car, angling the steering-wheel into the divet of his paunch. He started the car up and all but fishtailed it away. There were stars and stripes on the back numberplate, which read AVLANCH. Most likely there will be, but if there isn't, this may be the explanation – that there is nothing in the Republican armoury to match the grim and relentless phone banking of the Democrats' Organising For America outfit, and no right-wing gathering in this cycle has attracted even a fraction of the crowds turning out for Barack Obama. Whatever happens, AVLANCH will remain undisturbed in the towers of glass and steel. But who's stuck and who's pulling ahead. Columbus goodbye, hello.

5.

The SEIU Takes the Hilltop

columbus and the working poor,
wednesday 20 october

'That's where the GM plant used to be, been gone for years and years. Down here's Linda's house. There's three couples and then some, living there, two bedrooms. Can't afford the rent otherwise.' Late morning in Columbus, Ohio and Sandy, a middle-aged strong-armed blonde, with a raspy smoker's laugh, is showing me round Hilltop and 'The Bottoms', neighbourhoods she's lived in all her life. The place is pure Americana, wooden-verandahed houses between autumn trees, Halloween décor up, skeletons and pumpkins, fake cobweb under the windows. Every fourth or fifth house has an American flag sticking from it, though most are a little faded, one or two frayed. Two-storey wooden houses, mansard roofs, spacious family homes, they have the air of great calm, pure repose.

It looks like a good neighbourhood. In fact, it's a disaster area. Here at the corner of Fig and Eastgate, there's a well-kept place, new painted maroon, bright kids toys on the grass, a carpet hung out for beating. Next to it, there's an identical house painted white, with the wire screen door half hanging off. There's half a dozen notices pasted on the window – final demand, intention to repossess, twenty-eight day warning, form letters spat out of a printer, on a debt agency's two-colour letterhead. The letters are curled and rain-stained, and on the door there's a bright orange sheet taped down with black, announcing repossession and barring entry. There's another one on a house a few doors up the road. And one further up on this side, near a shuttered corner store. Sandy watches me taking a photo of the repossession notice, amused. 'Do you know who used to live here?' 'No idea,' she says, 'but I'm glad they're gone. They used to shoot at the house across the street.' 'They used to *shoot* at it.' 'Yeah,' she says, gurgling laughter again, 'they used to exchange fire.'

Sandy, and many of the people she knows across the area – 'that's Marcia's house; Ted lives over there' – might have worked at GM once, a long time ago. But that's all long gone. Now they work for Sodexo, the giant services conglomerate, which provides cleaners, canteen attendants and the like to schools, stadiums, and hospitals across the country. Sandy works in the food concession stands of the half-dozen stadia around the city. The property of the multi-billion dollar Ohio State University, the stadia host a dizzying array of college games, pro sports and concerts, and the money made on the stands is phenomenal – 'at the end of the day they haul the cash out in garbage bags'. As manufacturing has departed from Ohio, sports and events have taken up some of the slack.

But that shift to the entertainment-educational complex has come at a price – wages, conditions, respect. Sandy works all year round, with a few gaps. The job is food prep, kitchen cleaning, supply lugging, relentless, driving labour. In finals seasons it can run up to seventy hours a week, in back-to-back shifts, twelve hours on, six off, back for another twelve. Despite those hours, the job is listed as part-time, and most of the people who work there are denied permanent positions – which would oblige the company to offer them benefits, particularly health insurance. Having voted to join a union, the SIEU, the Hilltoppers are now fighting through the torturous process required to have their decision recognised by the company. It's part of a nationwide campaign by the SEIU, with pickets and demonstrations across the country. Sandy's been one of the most stalwart campaigners in Columbus, and she and Hayden, the quieter college-educated organiser are taking me on the tour of Hilltop they've been running for journalists for months. 'We give him the tour?' Sandy had said to

Hayden, after I'd met them at the SIEU's downtown headquarters. Hayden had smiled. 'Let's give him the tour.'

Three hours later I was finding out what that smile was for. I knew, of course. Any inquiry into the conditions of American working life in the post-manufacturing era is a passage into the badlands – the absurd, the grotesque, the crushing. Many people have been introduced to it by books such as Barbara Ehrenreich's *Nickel and Dimed*, her chronicle of trying to live on the minimum wage and falling short. By now we've become accustomed to the gap between working and living conditions for the low waged in the US on the one hand and just about everywhere else in the OECD, the stories of split shifts, two and three jobs, payday lending and foodstamps. You don't have to talk to many people in the US before you meet those whose lives will be forever lived in hock, on tick, one step from penury.

But fair go, nothing really prepared me for the trip into hell that morning, as Sandy took me through her life and that of her friends. As we drove around Hilltop, stopping off at the site of foreclosures, shootings, charity drops and low dives, it was as if one was descending the spiral path through the lower circles of suffering, every level revealing something worse.

'I get about seven bucks an hour,' Sandy says, as we turn back into the main street. 'It averages about two fifty a week. I'd earn more if I was permanent, but they're not going to give that to me now we're doing this. 'Stead they're running an attendance check on us, try and trip us up. You're three minutes late you get a warning. Happens twice written warning. Third time they can fire yer. Who isn't three minutes late?'

'You think they'd want all the workers they can get.'

'Nah, they're trying to get rid of us, replace us with volunteers.'

'Volunteers?'

'For the games involving college teams, community groups,' Hayden explains. 'They still fill the stadiums, but they're technically amateur. So they can crowd the paid staff out.'

'They let us have a few of the stands,' Sandy says. 'You know, we work hard on those stands. We given the company a lot of loyalty, now we want some back. Hey stop over here.' We pull up to a low slung building, plain brick, with a plastic awning.

'This here's the food pantry. I usually run out of money about the third week of the month, we come down here.'

'But this is not food stamps...'

'Naw, food stamps you use at the store...when we had a store. This is what they give out for free. You have to queue up at around five in the morning.'

'Five in the morning...but if you sometimes work seventy hours a week...'

'Yeah but it's not always seventy hours. See my old man's got MS, he's in a wheelchair, so we got costs...'

Already knowing the answer, I say: 'So he doesn't get any benefits...'

Sandy laughs again. It's not mocking, simply rueful.

'He don't get nothing...'

We check out the cheque-cashing joint, and the day labour centre – drab places, plastic chairs and lino, a couple of people waiting around. 'A lot of people get caught up in the cheque cashing thing. Ted eventually had to declare himself bankrupt.'

Hilltop's decline might be hidden by the sturdy build of its houses, but that doesn't work on Broad Street. You can still see the street it was, the deco facework and brick fronts of a street that was once the centre of a thriving community, a place where there was one of everything. Now half of them are closed or boarded up, and those still open have the air of squatted stores. A few are 'goodwill' emporia, charity shops of second hand furniture in what were once new furniture stores.

The food stores have a shabby air, their shelves half-filled. The local bar is a verandahed house, with a neon sign saying 'Mike's Place' out the front, and an old guy sitting on a beat-up armchair outside. It is unbelievably depressing. Sandy sees me looking at it. 'Yeah they had a big problem with prostitution out of there'. 'What did they do?' 'I think they changed the name.'

'Yeah I used to go there before I had my first heart attack...'

'Your first? How many have you had?'

'Two.'

'So what are you on?'

'Nothing – I mean I should be on Plavix but I can't afford it. Also I got to pay back the emergency room...'

'For...?'

'For my heart attacks. I mean they can't take your money if you got no money, but they send you a bill. Also they take my state tax rebate. I never see it. The government just sends it straight to them.' She thinks a second. 'Mind you, they don't charge for an ambulance, if it's an emergency.'

By now I had stopped writing. This had started as a local colour piece. It was turning into a war zone dispatch.

'So...'

'So people wait for an emergency to get care.'

'Doesn't Linda have heart disease as well?' Hayden asks.

'Yeah she splits medication with someone who has Medicaid. It's illegal but they do it. I just...hope.'

It's the first time that Sandy's bonhomie has faded a little. We get in the car and head a few blocks south.

'Where are we going?'

'Where my boy was killed.'

We get out at a rackety wooden house on a backroad. It's numbered 104 ½ in black felt-tip.

'My son was killed here,' Sandy says. 'He was shot. You can still see the bullet marks'. She points to two cracks in the wood, and a dint in the metal door.

'He saw a robbery happening down the street and shouted out. It stopped the robbery, but he was shot in the leg. It hit an artery and he bled out. I was upstairs. They tried to get in but he'd locked the door.'

She's quiet for a second. I look around. 'This happened at night?'

Sandy shakes her head. 'Middle of the day.'

Then: 'I gotta get to work.'

On the way to the stadium, we pass back beside the planed-flat lot where the GM plant once was. Nearby there's a billboard: 'Say yes to Hollywood' and a picture of a roulette wheel.

'They want a casino here?'

'Yeah, they got it – the Hollywood. It's going to open in '12,' Harley says. It got rejected a couple of times but they kept coming back with it. Eventually people supported it because they though it meant jobs.'

'Yeah, but they wont be employing locals,' Sandy says. 'They're going to bring in trained folks from Vegas and Atlantic City.' Apparently the US currently has a glut of trained croupiers.

'Where are they putting it?'

'Where the GM plant used to be.'

We drop Sandy at the stadium, the famous 'Horseshoe', part of one end open to the world. It is vast, cavernous, surreal, its sheer walls the height of a fifteen-storey building. It is the sixth largest in the world, the centrepiece of Ohio State University. The university is a vast multibillion dollar conglomerate, taking in whole neighbourhoods of Columbus, with a huge teaching hospital. Sodexo staffs its service positions throughout. The university doesn't want to know about any labour dispute.

After we'd dropped her off, I was standing in the car park for a few minutes reeling, while Hayden had a smoke. Sandy had probably got more knocks than most – but not too many more. Few people lose a child to gun violence, but many have health problems, many have sick people they're caring for, and many are living hand-to-mouth in post-industrial America. All the stuff that had hit Sandy could hit anyone – but anywhere else, these would not of themselves become a tragedy. In America, they are sufficient to throw her into the pit. She had found her freedom to a degree through her activism, lifting herself out of given circumstances, but that shouldn't be the only way in which to achieve a measure of humanity.

There is no end to the disaster that has befallen America, and no end to the fascination it provokes. It has happened so slowly, over decades, over the space of a whole lifetime. It has happened so slow that people have accepted it, for knowing nothing else. These cities, these places, were once whole and entire. In our passage through the suburbs of hell, I had asked Sandy what her parents had been. 'Well my mom worked in a school cafeteria, and my dad in a bakery. Worked there all their lives.' The family business, perpetuated. But of course her parents had not merely work but *jobs*, real, continuous occupations, turn up at nine leave at five, as part of ongoing institutions.

Twenty per cent of America lives like Sandy Dailey. Another ten per cent hovers just above it, forever fearing a fall into that world. A third of the population, the people who otherwise and elsewhere would have lives that did not need to be put together like patchwork, forever fighting the war against necessity. How did this happen? How did these cities, these powerhouses, these working and middle classes, how did they become destroyed and scattered, atomised and made prey to the vagaries of power, capital and media? Why have people accepted this so easily, so willingly? Why aren't they occupying buildings? Why aren't they burning them down?

More to the point, where, politically, will they go? Two years ago, many of them came out to elect Barack Obama. 'I voted for Obama but I'm not into politics...' Sandy remarks. But neither Obama nor the Democrats in Congress have delivered anything that would tangibly or concretely change Sandy's life now. At best, the healthcare bill would force her employers to provide a genuinely effective cheaper health insurance – though they could quite possibly still get around that by keeping her on permanent part-time work. TARP? The stimulus? Any effect those have had would be so removed and abstract as to make no difference at all. Tax credits? Sandy is below the line. Mandated transition to permanent status? The company would get around that, even if strong regulation around the casualisation of full-time work was instituted. Full public universal healthcare would have helped. The 'employee free choice act' – making unionisation less of an ordeal – would have helped, had it not been the first thing the Democrats gave up on.

Above all, better jobs would have helped. Big projects, infrastructure and housing, building shit, the sort of thing that could draw hundreds of thousands of different people into various different professions – and, of equal importance, into workplaces, where they can organise and unionise. The American working class has been so divided and scattered by the process of deindustrialisation, globalisation and social destruction that benefits flow very unevenly. Even the bailout and salvation of GM has had little positive impact in a state like Ohio, traditionally the place where decentralised autoparts manufacturers are established. Though some existing jobs across the state will be saved, the direct benefits to working people will flow principally to the relatively small core of workers involved in full body auto production.

There remains great and solid support for the Democrats within this shrunken industrial heart. Today, Nancy Pelosi addressed the United Steelworkers, and if they felt that this botoxed and coiffed scion of planet Frisco was not one of them, they didn't show it, and nor did she. In these parts, the American liberal–worker coalition survives. But it diminishes in near exact proportion to the distance of workers from – well, from work. From workplaces to which they return each day, where they are unionised, where collective existence abides across time and space. By destroying their cities and abolishing permanent full-time work, capital scattered these people in both directions. Some, like Sandy, regroup – both out of their own determination and the fact that a workplace of sorts remains, where identity and information has ways of being shared other than by media and the marketplace. But the further you go into the outer circles – into the day labour centres, the nothing world of cashless unemployment – the more that a political determination fades, like the flags on the porches.

There is no space in the media for the most basic issues in people's lives. Today, the talk was all of the New York governors' debate, the campaign already a freak show courtesy of Republican candidate Carl Paladino, a Buffalo businessman fond of sharing the occasional bestiality porn clip with employees, and threatening to have a reporter 'taken out'. The debate, open to all comers, turned it into a circus, with a former madam Kristin Davis favourably comparing her own business to the transit authority ('at least we make people happy'), the star being Jimmy McMillan, a grandly tonsured black man and serial candidate, this time running on 'the rent is too damn high', both the name of his party, its entire platform, and pretty much the whole of his contribution – a wordslam poetic series of variations: rent is too DAMN high, rent is too damn HIGH, can you hear the people saying, you got to listen like me, rent is too damn HIGH.

The clip was replayed endlessly, to much bonhomie, with barely an acknowledgement that not merely in New York but everywhere, the rent *is* too damn high. 'I'm paying a hundred a week now,' Sandy had told me. 'Coupla years ago I was paying a hundred and fifty. I really couldn't afford that. I was down at the food pantry by the second week of the month.' With little public accommodation, at the mercy of landlords price-fixing in concert, rent can eat up fifty to seventy per cent of a minimum wage, for houses that could once hold whole families on a single adult wage, now packed to the faux-gothic roofs, slowly flaking and blowing away.

'What should Obama have done?' I ask Hayden at the end of it all, as he drops me at the three-star chain motel, a basic place, two nights at which would consume Sandy's weekly salary entire.

'Oh I think we needed a new deal, a bailout of main street. That would have done it.'

Damn right. Obama should have rolled a barrel of pork all the way down to the Bottoms, and split it open with an axe. Had he done so, he would have himself an army. Instead, here we are at the top of the hill, with a vacant lot where the plant used to be, and everyone hoping for a place in the new casino.

6.

Obama Nirvana in Seattle

stumping in washington state,
thursday 21 october

'Now what you've all been waiting for...' In the Huskies basketball stadium, all regal purple banners and white-painted girders, they're already on their feet and cheering, before the MC can finish the sentence 'would you please welcome...'. Ten thousand people steeply banked to the ceiling, students, Seattle folk, out-of-towners, some from Canada ('dude, he's not even your President'). The kids are freshers and sophomores, girls with brown hair and baby fat, guys with college tops and peach-fuzz. The adults? Farmers, ex-hippies, old draft dodgers, dockers, timberworkers. Short hair and salt-and-pepper ponytails, grey sweats and Jimi Hendrix tie-dye.

Up in the gods, there's half a dozen guys in t-shirts for 'Rossi', the challenger, standing in a wall, politely ignored. Everyone else is holding shining red signs for Senator Patty Murray, 'helping people solve problems', the room's a spray of blood. We've had two hours of the usual for a stadium appearance, one-hour wait time, a nu-style gospel choir – 'Amazing Grace', 'Somebody To Lean On' – Congressman Jim Ansley, who played for the college team, 'go huskies', huge roar, another Congressman, an old Irish dock-bar fighter, and Christine Gregoire, the state's junior senator.

We'd started with the Pledge of Allegiance and Star-Spangled Banner, the type of revolutionary anthem I'd give my left hand to be able to put my right hand over my heart for. Country rock filled the gap, aural Starbucks, functional and inoffensive. The Mexican waves had a langorous air, folks throwing up one hand, without getting up or even shifting in their seat, much.

But now it's the main event, and all reserve goes. The signs wave furiously, the diminutive Murray bounces on stage, and Obama follows her in an impossibly crisp white shirt. After a tilt to the crowd, 'wassup Seattle!' and the roar back, he has to stand tilted towards Murray listening attentively as she gives the spiel. Barely able to be seen over the podium, she's nevertheless in command. 'Volunteer at the phonebank, walk the precinct...update your Facebook status page!'

The 'senator in tennis shoes' – an old community activist, she was elected to a school board and kept on going – has a fight on her hands for the first time since taking office in 1992. Though she's regarded as a tireless worker for the state and its people, the anti-Obama, anti-Pelosi, anti-incumbent wave has hit her hard. She's a victim of what is shaping up to be the main story of the election – the enthusiasm gap. A Pew poll out this week shows that of people who class themselves as Republicans, 64% are interested and focused on this election. The figure for Democrats is 49%. That 15% gap is killing, and is obscured by the fact that Obama can pull out crowds like no one else. But even a full stadium doesn't go head to head with hundreds of thousands of folks sitting at home, watching FOX News more than they used to, quietly sharpening their pencils.

A *New York Times* CBS poll paints a yet grimmer picture. Obama and the Democrats have lost vast amounts of support in a whole range of key demographics: among those earning under fifty thousand a year, support has swung from 22% above even, to 2% below; among college grads, from evens to 20% down; among women, from 12% above to minus 4%, and, crucially, among independent voters from 7% up to 20% down. A college-educated woman, middle income and of independent mind – if that isn't a picture of the Pacific Northwest, what is? And hence the desperate struggle for survival is now.

Rossi's a former senator in the state assembly, and head of ways and means. Balancing the budget in 2002 gave him a reputation for bipartisanship, which he's now running hard away from, trumpeting his low-tax, anti-abortion credentials. Patty Murray beat back all comers by ten per cent or more each previous time out. She campaigned for and got student grants, for and got big air force contracts, for and got a clean-up of Puget Sound. Through the 90s and 2000s she was seen as Washington state first and Democrat second by a lot of people who wouldn't have much time for the likes of her otherwise.

But now she's leading by one or two per cent. Washington state would be a disastrous loss for the Democrats, and the past week has seen Bill Clinton, Joe Biden and now Obama come through town. This last one's the best. The atmos is near embarrassing. Kids are shouting out 'I love you Barack!'

'Well, I love you too,' he tells them back, on the third go. He's filled out a little since oh eight; there were times that year when he looked twenty-six. Now, there's more heft, and some grey in the tight curls of his hair. Speech-wise, he's broadened also. Either his impossibly young writing team got tougher, or others were drafted in, because this is a harder sell than any I heard last time around. He begins by rousing them up – 'everyone's telling us, no we can't, and you're saying...' and the crowd roars back, 'yes we can'. That's only to let them down:

'When I took office we were losing three hundred, five hundred thousand jobs a month. We lost eight million jobs before my economic plan even got started. I hoped that when I got to Washington we could put aside our differences work together...we're proud to be Democrats but prouder to be Americans!'

Big roar on that, but:

'The Republicans want to pretend they had nothing to do with it. The Republicans are betting on amnesia. Seattle it's up to you to tell them you haven't forgotten. '

After that, he's got a shaggy dog story, a two line gag – 'The Republicans drove the car into the ditch, we got it out, now they want the keys back' – which he's turned into a five-minute extravaganza. 'An' we're down there, Patty Murray and I in the ditch, and Patty's small but she's strong, and the Republicans are up there on the road, telling us we're getting their car out wrong...'

For this crowd, it goes over hugely, but he steps on the punch line a little, his conviction failing perhaps. Maybe he's done this sort of thing as a community organiser, but it sounds more like an adopted Bill Clinton style, to get him out of the realm of abstraction and wonkery.

'See it's just like in a car – you hit the "D" when you want to go forward and the "R" when you want to go in reverse!'

Another huge roar. So why the hell didn't they use a simple image like that in the campaign, in the ads? It's a great non-sequitur, like the line by Tea Party women – Sharron Angle, Christine O'Donnell – to their opponents to 'man up', or, even better, 'get your man-pants on'. There's only two responses to that: either 'why don't you grow a brain you dangerous psycho-bimbo' or pure spluttering.

Pure spluttering is, sadly, what the Democrats do well these days. For months they have left a vacuum where advocacy politics should be. Now, with this barnstorming tour, they appear to be in a desperate attempt to make up ground that they suddenly realise is not merely lost but yawning beneath their feet. That failure, that catastrophic failure, cannot but add a slight tang of bitterness to seeing the One working the stadium here. A recent *Rolling Stone* report sums it up effectively, quoting a poll showing that only 12% of Americans know that Obama had delivered them a tax cut as part of the stimulus; 24% thought he had raised them. In response to this statistic, the magazine got one of the most revealing quotes of the election from David Axelrod, who remarked: 'We've focused on trying to build a better country for the future – the president's attitude is the politics will ultimately take care of itself.' To be fair, not every Democrat has decided to go gentle into that good night. Some of them are fighting back, though not without the occasional edge of desperation. In Kentucky, the opponent of Tea Party-endorsed Senate candidate Rand Paul (son of Ron), has launched an ad which attacks Paul for denouncing Christianity at college, and 'forcing a handcuffed woman to bow to an idol he called 'Aqua Boodha'. Cue 60s imagery of a green buddha, trance-like visions.

It's a measure of what is acceptable to the Kentucky electorate that the Democrats have reached for this stuff, since nothing else about Paul would dissuade them. Like his father, Rand Paul believes that the Federal Reserve should be abolished, and that the US should return to the gold standard. Previously, he had stated that he would not have voted for the 1964 Civil Rights Act, because it made discrimination by private firms illegal. The college antics were a few antinomian pranks that occurred when he was attending the strictly Christian Baylor University, and joined a skullnbones-style society. But it was possibly the only thing that might have had a chance of sowing some doubt as to his bona fides at the heart of the Bible belt.

More on the money was an ad in Connecticut, aimed at Republican Senate candidate Linda McMahon, a former CEO of WWE, the cartoonish TV wrestling franchise. Like Meg Whitman and numerous other candidates, McMahon was funding her own campaign – a trend that may ultimately prove more significant to politics than the Tea Party, the growth of plutocracy in America. McMahon's opponent Richard Blumenthal ran an ad that slated McMahon for imposing independent contractor work agreements on the 'wrestlers', so as to avoid the health care costs associated with their practically necessary steroid use. WWE-style, Blumenthal's head beats McMahon over the head with a chair, accusing her of profiting from their early death. Effectively combining labour issues and postmodern spectacle, it's a tough and effective intervention

That such has been lacking at the very head of the party is why Obama needs to be here in this stadium now, and mid-speech, deploying the whole campaign finance thing, and then moving onto the argument from failure: 'the Republicans say they want to do the exact same thing that already failed. Nothing is more certain than that that would fail again'. Then getting out the volunteers: 'because of what you did last time, people don't have to choose which medicine to buy; because of you more kids will go to college, because of you...and if as many people vote in this election as last we will win!'.

By which he means, of course, lose less badly than presumed, and retain both Houses. He ends with the Revolution, and its triumph through audacity: 'thirteen colonies, if they'd listened to the doubters it never would have happened, we wouldn't be here! The slaves wouldn't have been freed, women wouldn't have gained equal rights'. The cheering starts, and it ramps up, and by the time he's urging everyone to make a hundred phone calls and walk a precinct, we can't hear him but we know what he's saying.

He exits, working the barrier. The crowd keeps waving a sea of placards. The sign-language interpreters, in the stands not on stage, lean back exhausted. The pool press descend on the crowd, notebooks in hand. More country rock, 'Only in America' by Brooks and Dunn from 2001, enough description for you to know it without hearing it ever, and the morning's one concession to this exceptionalism, the crack habit of American politics.

Out in the University grounds, I look for the Dino Rossi boys, but they've gone. There's the LaRouchites, with their Obamahitler posters, and their 'Biden 2010 – impeach Obama' posters, but I don't want to kill the buzz. Beside the stadium, the wheelchair-bound, the becrutched, the dog-led blind ('don't pet me, I'm at work' the sign reads) are getting out first.

I pick a black kid. Cameron, in a wheelchair with an Obama t-shirt, being wheeled out by his mom, Robin. 'I work in telecoms, my husband in sales'. And has anything Obama's done made a difference?' Oh yes, now insurers can't exclude us for a pre-existing condition.' I'm conscious I'm talking across the kid. I ask him 'what do you want to do when you leave school?' 'Ah, I don't know.' 'And if you don't mind me asking what is your condition?' Robin prompts him, gently, 'tell him.' 'Muscular dystrophy.' Damn damn damn. Second question should have been first, and the first question wouldn't have been asked.

Should the healthcare bill be repealed, they would sell their house as Cameron's condition worsened, and declare bankruptcy when the funds ran out. There would be better ways to assuage this than mandating insurance, with a more perfect healthcare bill, but perhaps this comes down to the good and bad compromises thing. For some there is no waiting. They are the people. Their time is now.

7.

Celebration Time At Sarah Palin's Magic Kingdom

orlando, florida,
saturday 23 october

'Give me your heart, make it real or else forget about it...' Festooned with 'Fire Pelosi' and 'Listen To Me' posters and banners, and the phat sounds of a good old boys band – 'This Magic Moment', 'Smooth' ('Give Me Your Heart, Make It Real') – bouncing off the walls, the Cypress Room of the Marriott World Centre, Orlando, was on fire. Before a stage filling with Florida dignitaries and candidates glad-handing each other, a crowd of 500 or so were milling around, admiring each others' gloriously wacky get-up.

Mere patriotism didn't make the grade here. A stars and stripes shirt was par for the course. Stars and stripes and a screaming eagle across your left nipple, that was getting there. But to stand out, you really needed the full get-up – screaming eagle shirt, shoulder bag with the Declaration of Independence dyed in, foam Statue of Liberty halo, with a flag stuck out the back of it. A slogan helped. 'Jesus if you're not coming back soon could you send Ronald Reagan' was my favourite. Everyone I could see was white, oldish and sprawling, except the liveried staff darting about, young and thin and brown. There were going to be speeches soon, from every local gomer, but the crowd was here for one reason only. Palin, the divine Sarah, making her final appearance of the campaign, a week out from the vote, preserving her mystery to the last. In true Republican style, this was somewhere between a rally and a fundraiser.

Everyone here in the bullpen had paid twenty bucks to get in. Those sitting in a roped-off area to one side had shelled out a couplahundred. Somewhere at the front, there were a dozen or so people who'd paid nine hundred and fifty dollars, for the privilege of a photo with the woman herself afterwards. They waved balloons and flags and ate ice-cream. They looked like they were having a pretty good time. The band wound up 'Old Time Rock n Roll' with a flourish. 'Now here's something you're going to love,' the lead guitarist said, the drummer began a cymbal wash, and the singer leant in to start: 'I see trees of green...', he croaked, in pure satchmo imitation. Yeah, they loved that. A cheer went up. None of that 'Give Me Your Heart' punk shit. Real music, and a white guy imitating a black guy, and nothing anyone can say about it. Doesn't get any better than that. Where's that ice-cream?

Palin's appearance here was capping off the penultimate week of the campaign, and she had nothing further scheduled. Despite all the hoopla, to use one of her favourite words, her appearances have to be carefully managed to give the impression that she's a national phenomenon, when she's not. Obama can fill stadiums. Palin can't even fill a ballroom at this vast conference centre in the heart of Florida's Disney country. Wandering out to avoid the remainder of the band's minstrel show, I look down corridor after corridor of function rooms. Next door has an investment seminar, there's a realtors' meeting down the hall in the Anaheim room, and in the atrium there's no one, save for a blind man tuning a grand piano.

The place feels like an arcade of private obsessions, discreet and entire of themselves, all scheduled for 4-6, before the next wedding reception. When you open the door to re-enter the Palin rally, the energy and enthusiasm spills out, but only for a metre or so. The band's already wrapped it up, someone's speaking. Sounds like they're halfway through the candidate roster already. 'Most people think agricultural commissioner doesn't matter...' Good god, it's the same speech. Everywhere. The mood in the room was even more impatient, like kids queueing for a ride. Where's Sarah? 'Now someone who needs no introduction...' finally, and the band strike up, and there's that flash of red jacket as she comes out to huge cheering, people really losing it.

'We're here for the hard-working god-fearing small-town down-home time-tested truths that can be applied for all time...'. My god she is something, Palin. Always the flame red outfit, the hair piled, high, the glasses. She's a walking logo. The jaw line is spare and thin, either from sheer energy, or bulimia ('Hetherrr'). More likely the former. She goes up like a rocket, and keeps on going. We'd already had Senate candidate Marco Rubio, the Tea Party favourite who'd beaten governor Charlie Crist to the Republican nomination, rallying the crowd with the plaintive cry 'Is America just going to be like any other nation?' 'No! We're unique in history!' But nothing got them going like Palin.

'And you know it's that exceptionalism that Ronald Reagan talked about and people ask us why we keep referring back to Reagan and not you know Alinsky or Ayres and you know you gotta put in the hours cos it's that exceptionalism that Reagan talked about...'. There's no way to transcribe or notate a Sarah Palin speech that in any way captures its effect or appeal. The voice has the tenor of an electric sander and the rhythmic discipline of the Sun Ra orchestra. She hits a note that takes the top of your ear off, and then she goes up in thirds. Her prose evokes Whitman at times, but more often monster truck rallies, clauses smashing in until one rides over the other and prevails.

'Our country is at a tippling point talk about a do-over needed hit the re-set button'

And then there's the sarcasm. 'There's something about this lady that drives the liberal press wild,' the MC had said and he was spot on. There's always a middle part of every Palin stump speech when she starts to lay it on thick beyond thick, with a toxic turbocharged mix of sarcasm, irony and contempt. There's nothing real witty about it, but it pins you screaming to the wall.

'You know they talk about the stimulus but ykkknnnnnnow, let's just look at some of the things they were stimulating you betcha like a let's see two million dollar study to see the effects of drunkenness on mice...oh my he deception...please don't anyone tell Obama what number comes above a trillion yknnnoww yknnowwwww'

What can you say to that? Nothing, nothing at all, because there's nothing to reply to – and in any case, the next four clauses have already arrived. The mind can't regroup, and two, three, four punches and you're down, wondering, 'what happened? What happened?'. By now, everyone who's heard Palin's spiel has remarked on it, with no real hope of getting it out of their head. You love it if you're behind it, watching your enemies squirm, but what makes it so remarkable? It's high school stuff of course, and most of the pain comes from regression – for guys, it's being outwitted by girls, for girls, it's being outwitted by cooler girls. Two sentences of Palin, and you're back in the year 11 locker room, getting a free personality analysis from Stacey, who goes out with a footballer.

One suspects that this schtick is deadly because it is so new to political discourse. Since women began entering mainstream politics in significant numbers two decades ago they have, in general, adopted one of three rhetorical modes – either mature and rising above the boys games, or hyper-aggressive and playing it better than the men, or occasionally, a la Thatcher, adopting a terrifying matronly tone. The one thing they've steered clear of is girlishness, and bitchiness. It's that note that Palin has made her own. In her mid-forties, she hasn't come through the second-wave women's movement like Hillary Clinton, or the corporate world like Carly Fiorina. Having floated through five universities – the one and only thing she has in common with George Steiner, apart of course from writing essays on Holderlin – following her galpals, before landing a job in Alaskan sportscasting, her whole life has been spent in the Breakfast Club, sizing up the competition. Though she may have been played for a dupe during the McCain campaign, that's over. Others are writing her words, but the style is all her own, a political invention. Marshalled against the portentous, and sometimes vacuous, appeal to depth made by Obama, she deploys the same tone of high-school, the idea that none of this study stuff matters, that it is all illusion. Depthlessness alone is real.

The Marriott World Centre couldn't be a better place to expound this philosophy. It stands high on the plain, vast, as if entirely made from cardboard fifteen minutes ago. It hosts conferences, conventions, exhibitions. They come from the airport, they arrive, stay, go. They are in nothing, near nothing, bordering on nothing. The Orlando zone – it is by no stretch of the term a city – was a centre of 'crops and pro-doose' until Disney opened its second and largest theme park here in 1971. Now there's a dozen theme parks, from the original Disneyworld to Seaworld to Disney Hollywood Orlando. They all needed workers, and so the fantasy parks led a boom in real estate, which then became a boom of its own. Along the freeways subdivisions rear up from the brilliant green of the scrub pine. Currently, not only are many of the houses empty, but so too are whole subdivisions – ghost suburbs, their gates open, each house perfectly unmarked and unindividuated, awaiting owners who may now never come. At some point, Disney itself noted the money to be made from real estate and got into the game. At that point the circle closed – a fantasy-led recovery became an entire fantasy economy. People whose day job was to dress as either Snow White or one of the Seven Dwarfs were buying houses in places developed on the basis of developments created with negative money down, with an absence of money, bundled as future security against further debt, which would be used to create the next development. But Disney being Disney, mere tract housing was insufficient. They wanted something more. And lo the result was Celebration.

Celebration, the faux-Americana town that Disney made in the late 1990s – and then sold off – sits close to the original theme park and takes its spirit from it. I'd made a deal with a cab driver to take me on a round trip from the Marriott World, effectively fitting the whole town into a gap in the Palin afternoon schedule. On the map it was just around the corner, which entailed a twenty-minute drive through more scrub and subdivisions, all rolling forward like a loop in a drive simulator. The radio played bossa nova, interspersed with political ads:

'Hi,' said an elderly female voice, 'I'm Rick Scott's mom – Rick never got anything for anyone that he didn't earn.'

'What the hell is this?' I asked the driver.

'Oh that guy's running for governor.'

'With an endorsement from his mom?'

'Yeah,' the driver chuckled. 'The guy used to run a health conglomerate. He hadda resign after it turned out they were bilking Medicare. Never got anything he didn't earn hah!'

By now we were turning into the main entrance to Celebration, with a sudden efflorescence of vine-clad verandahs, doric columns, and lemon-painted clapboard. There's a functioning main street, a tiny fountain in the main square, a lake and small waterfront. The lake featured in *The Truman Show*, in which Celebration played the home town Truman was programmed never to leave. That would make it weird under any circumstance, but it's only when you get deeper into the centre that you see how utterly, utterly strange Celebration is.

For Celebration is more than a housing development made to imitate a certain period of American life. Amid the flag-swept lawns, and white paling fences, there's an old-style grain tower housing the Bank of America. There's a post-office with a circular entrance hall, in the style of the deco post offices built during the New Deal and after. There's a red-brick city hall, with a high narrow-timbered portico, after the Lloyd-Wright/Scandinavian fad of the 60s, a style still recent enough to be ugly. But of course it's all evocative of the sort of places folks here grew up in, and that is Celebration's weirdest effect – it is an instantaneous evocation of a layered, historied, less than perfect American small town.

Down near the lake it was even weirder, for the clapboard style had been lent to a larger series of buildings more accommodating to spacious restaurants and the like. They had several storeys and towers, wide bay windows to look across the water. There were bars with street furniture, cafes, tiny gelateria. People were sitting out eating yet more ice-cream. In the midst of Americana, it was the most European place I had seen. 'Yeah it's a nice place,' said Gracie, who runs a bar there. 'We lived outside for ten years, moved in last year. Before that we were in Baton Rouge.' She smiled. 'That's not like

Celebration.' Outside of another bistro, two kitchenhands who wouldn't give their names, even false ones, laughed when I asked whether they lived here. 'We commute.'

The place was impossible to assimilate. Real people taking their kids for a day out looked like expert actors. A pumpkin patch being run by the local Presbyterian Church was a splash of orange against the sky, impossibly orange, a meta-orange. I picked up a local paper from a rack. It was called 'Community'. Beside it was Brad, a buff guy in a Lakers shirt. And beside Brad was his Segway, the only civilian one I've ever seen, being held like a faithful pony.

'Yeah I love it here,' he said, the lakelight flashing off his shades. 'They've really kept it nice'. But I understood that there were a lot of building controls, very tight planning laws. 'Oh yeah, you can't do a thing here, can't paint your door without permission. But you gotta do that.' And what, if he didn't mind me asking, were his politics? 'Oh I'm a conservative. I really believe we've got to let the free market restart the recovery.'

I told the driver I would be another ten minutes, and went for a walk beside the lake. I tried to imagine living here. Everything about it was the sort of place I liked – sensuous living materials for the buildings, a uniformity of style without a monotony, an openness to the street and to the coming-and-going of foot traffic, for the chance encounter with known people whose lives yours is bound up with. Which is, after all, community.

But of course it would be torment. Most people would imagine it to be such. Indeed, a judgement as to whether Celebration represented heaven or hell may well be a fundamental division between human beings. But why? It is scarcely the first ever pre-fabricated community, and there is no reason to believe its original intent would dominate its life going into the future. After all, suburbs themselves are creations of the 'garden city' movement, the idea that country and city should commingle, on the basis of all sorts of batty theories about human nature. Why does Celebration feel so airless? And does it never occur to its planners and inhabitants that this image of America is only maintained by the sort of restrictions on liberty – in the matter of how you deal with your own property – that would have your average Swede or Amsterdamer going 'oh come onnnnnn'. Will the quasi private-public corporations cause Celebration to mimic America in time as well at space? Will they, at some point, stage urban riots here, and then flatten the whole city centre and replace it with a concrete conference centre and multistorey car park?

The question is the answer. Celebration only works as an evocation of Americana because at some point in history, *it rules off*. Its most 'recent' building, its early 60s city hall, stops where America stopped as a community, at Johnson's 'Great Society'. What came after that was urban decay, decline, demolition and dislocation, the transformation of community into 'development', of place into real estate. Tellingly, Celebration is lacking in all the most distinctive features of American urban or town life, the things that tell you you're in the US: boarded-up shops, a tattoo parlour, a Food Lion in a flatroof 70s building, vacant lots of buildings torn down to avoid property tax. To some degree, Celebration would be more accurately named Mourning. It can see a past for America, but no future, and it can admit little of the present. It sees no possibility that 'community' can be achieved by any process other than invoking its prior forms.

Thinking this, I looked over the lake. This is the place of the key scene in *The Truman Show,* its best and worst moment. Having realised that his whole life and community is a lie, Truman decides to set out for the real world, which lies across the lake.

We know from backstory that the producers of the series based around his life have conditioned him with a fear of water – so that he remains content to stay within the bounds of Celebration. He takes a yacht and sails the lake. Reaching the other side, the prow of the yacht bursts the outer skin of the vast studio in which his world is maintained – the film's most uncanny moment. There the film effectively ends. Because of course it can no further. After all, what happens to Truman next? He has lived all his life in a closed community, the sort of community that people have lived in throughout the history of the species. Now, he is out among America, the whole mad boiling of it, the vast anti-community. What will become of him? He will fall apart of course. Though the movie believes itself to be a tribute to individuality, a celebration of it, in fact it exposes the incoherence of the idea. Truman can't go back to Celebration because he knows it to be a false construct. But it is impossible to imagine him going forward either, without complete and utter collapse. That tearing of the studio skin, the rupture by the yacht's prow, is a register of that impossibility. It is a rupture in his imaginary world, the sudden intrusion of the real, which remains ungraspable, unassimilable.

Forget *The Truman Show*. What one longs for is *Truman Two*, the sequel. In this film Truman, after living for a few years off the celebrity of being an escaped reality show character, has now entered a decline. He has lived the high life, made millions, married and divorced a porn star, appeared on other reality shows. But now it's over, and he's adrift, lacking context, lacking meaning. One night, in desperation, he sneaks back to the vast studio where the Truman Show was made. The 'lake' has been drained now, so he walks back across its dry bed to Celebration. He imagines that it will be deserted, but still intact. But he is surprised to find that he is not the only one there. Some of the actors from the series have returned. Nothing in their subsequent life has even remotely lived up to the intensity, the immediacy, the meaning and presence of pretending to be part of a community. Faced with echt America as it is, they have one by one returned to Celebration, and made their own sort of community there. They've torn down some of the faux-town houses for fuel, and they've ploughed up the ornamental gardens to sow crops. It's tough, but they're making a go of it. In this abandoned studio, amid the clapboard and white paling of this abandoned meme, they feel right. They feel real.

It's either that, or Truman has joined the Tea Party. That would mark the final stage of his journey. He's living in a condo, working as a FOX News commentator and turning up to meetings of people in tricorn hats, raving about Ronald Reagan and the twentyeleventh amendment. This baroque weave of fantasy and reality – it's the place where Sarah Palin is, what she's talking about. Celebration is the content of her speeches. It's the America people stopped building some time ago, living on in memory and bullshit. So close to Celebration, there's some irony in Palin's relentless rah-rah. For her evocation of an exceptional America, living off an eternal flame, serves the same purpose as Celebration, the meticulous re-creation of a past moment.

Five minutes early, the driver honked, as prearranged. The airport was the other side of Orlando, which was like being in another state.

'Can't stand that place,' he said, as we hit the open road. At 'Maingate East', the entrance to Celebration, where the staff come in to work at community, the highway was littered with the usual fast food and big box outlets out the edge of every town. They may have been drawn there by the growing population, but they could have been meticulously planned by Disney to mimic post-urban planning. It was impossible to tell.

'How long have you been in Orlando?'

'Twenty years. I was a building contractor until a year ago before you ask. I folded the company up and paid out my staff last year rather than go under.'

'The place seems a little quiet.'

'It's shut down. Shut down. This has the second worst new home foreclosure rate in the country. If you don't live by the beach, you're paying off a home worth a third of its value. Everyone's walked out on their mortgages.'

'Has *anyone* stayed?'

'Only schmucks.'

At Orlando airport, Palin's triumphant appearance was being broadcast on every screen. The airport had a hotel in its centre atrium. You could go on holiday here, and never leave departure/arrivals. This I plan to do at some point in my life, a tiny celebration. Gales of children were being herded by adults towards the exit. Some of them were in wheelchairs or coloured beanies, make-a-wish kids. In the parking bay, they all queued at a sign that said 'Magic Kingdom Shuttle', and, more calmly than one would have expected, waited for the bus. Come back Ronald, come back Truman, come back Jesus. Forget about it, make it real, give me your heart.

8.

Leaving New Haven

random notes on the
new england line, tuesday 25 october

'Leaving New Haven, we are leaving New Haven...'

Last week, Levi Johnston, on *The View*, the ladies around him, male stripper at worst hen-party ever: 'are you still running for mayor? Republican or democrat?' 'Conservative.' 'Have you ever voted?' Silence. 'I haven't even started campaigning yet.' 'Is it true you were going to do it as a reality TV show?' Silence.

In a Newark bar, ESPN talking of a footballer paralysed from neck down. His coach: 'he's going to be hearing a lot of negatives, so today we're giving him positives.'. In other news the Cowboys have been penalised for 'excessive celebration'.

Meaghan McCain is on the Rachel Maddow show. Our host has just interviewed Christopher Hayes from *The Nation*, who looks even more like a lesbian graduate student than Maddow does. McCain jeune fille drawls on about Christine O'Donnell: oh like she's a nut job, none of my friends like her. She and Maddow snicker together. How did one of the nation's leading liberal commentators come to think it would be a good idea to laugh at a suburban candidate, with a grandee Republican airhead? Explains much.

69

'Dave Thomas changed the image of fast food by serving it hot off the grill in a clean and comfortable setting, all part of Dave's founding principle of service...' – metal sign at the site of the first Wendy's, Columbus, Ohio. It's now a vacant lot.

On basic cable tonight: *Kill Bill 1 and 2*, *Entourage*, the *40 Year Old Virgin*. Fantasies of success, of violence, but it is the last of these that repays reviewing, a tale of mall-based inadequacy, of non-sex as refusal of being in the game. The movie portrays the relentless sexual hermeneutics of Steve Carrell's co-workers as funny, self-deprecating but only to more effectively portray the savagery of it. It's really the film version of Houellebecq's *Whatever* (*Extension de la domaine de la lutte*) – his argument that the principal result of the 60s was to extend atomistic capitalist competition to the world of love, sex and intimacy, to make us finally and utterly alone.

On CNN, an identikit Republican fembot who claims to represent the Tea Party gives her take on the 'no establishment clause for religion' of the first amendment: 'well you know secularism is a religion, music's a religion to some people, why pick on Christianity?' Amazingly she is not instantly drowned out by laughter.

'Did Rand Paul, while in college, force a handcuffed naked woman to kneel before an idol he called 'Aqua Buddha?'. The ad is being endlessly repeated far from Kentucky. 'Why does he worship false images?' Yes, because that is the most worrying thing about that event. The woman later comes forth to say it's fine, it was just college.

Half a day's news cycle is taken up with revelations that one of California gubernatorial democratic candidate Jerry Brown's staff called opponent Meg Whitman 'a whore'. Not in a speech, not publicly, but in a private campaign meeting caught on tape. The state, the fifteenth largest economy in the world, is broke. It has been broke for three years. The least-liked man in California politics? Arnold Schwarzenegger, greeted as some sort of avatar at the time of his election, before shedding his Terminator-skin to reveal a European-style centrist.

Mentioned during the Illinois Senate debate: the Jesus Name Apostolic Church Smarties Programme.

Glenn Beck. FOX News at 5pm everyday. The performance is by now utterly mannered, baroque, rococo. The stage is strewn with blackboards, charts, a desk piled with books. There's the air of a weary history teacher in Des Moines c.1949, explaining the communist menace. 'Ygotta hah ygotta shake of the head ygotta understand what's really going on...'

On *The View*, Elizabeth Hasselback introduces the next segment, on cancer. She's off to have her tiny episcopalian breasts mammogrammed. She brings along a black crew member, whose bazongas are too big for the machine.

Man-up. Get your man-pants on. Sharron Angle and Christine O'Donnell to their male opponents, launching a thousand cultural studies dissertations.

My girlfriend comes over from England for a few days, her first time in the US. She reminds me by her amazement of how amazing the pharma ads are. 'Side effects may include dizziness nausea, backache cramps. In some rare cases paralysis has been reported. Stroke cerebral haemorrhage instant death is not unknown.' Guitar music plays under throughout. The pharma ads alternate with insurance pitches. Illness and danger. Advertising, the science of creating new desires, has become the principal agent in the manufacture of new fears. This utterly divides the US from any other nation, and determines its character.

Mark Kirk, Illinois GOP candidate: 'I would have voted for [supreme court judge] Elena Kagan, but Sonia Sotomayor would be too...forward leaning for me.'

'Forward Leaning, MSNBC'. The liberal network has adopted the oft-used conservative criticism as its proud slogan, despite the fact that it is blatheringly meaningless.

Joan Rivers on *Fashion Police*: 'Jennifer Aniston oh her skirts are way too short it's like she's saying "I could have dinner and a pap smear at the same time". She's got to do better movies. In the last one that dog was begging to die.'

An ad for 'cancer treatment centres of America', a private health franchise. It features a woman who runs a store and had pancreatic cancer. She tells, sobbing, of how her first doctor tells her to go home to the store, and, implicitly, die. 'There was no compassion.' She then went to CTCA and they said 'we did all sorts of tests on you and I never saw any stamp on your foot that said 'going to die'. A crawl across the screen: 'results are not typical. You should not expect this diagnosis.' The pancreatic cancer survival rate? Two per cent. It would be more moral to sell diluted penicillin to children than the idea that bedside manner will cure an internal organ cancer.

Sharron Angle on tape in a bizarre encounter at a Nevada school, telling a bunch of Hispanic 11-year-olds: 'some of you look Asian to me'.

Karl Rove tells *Der Spiegel*: 'the Tea Party are not sophisticated...it's not like they've read Hayek or anything.'

Beck: rails about currency destruction, urges the gold standard. Cut to an ad for gold sales. Comes back, talks about Soros. Imitates Soros's mitteleuropean accent. Goes over to a puppet-theatre, and manipulates two marionettes, while talking about the collapse of the US dollar in a Sorosian accent. It skirts the edge of mid-twentieth century antisemitism without falling into it.

Don't stop believin': that used to be a great song, a suburban loser anthem. Streetlight people. Bad exercise-book poetry. Now it's everywhere. Someone used it for Bush's departure in Marine One, on inauguration day. That was bad enough, but then *Glee* got hold of it, and it was all over.

Sherry, in the Newark airport Days Inn. She's from St Louis. Her birthday, she keeps getting calls from friends and greetings on Facebook, which she keeps open on her Droid. She organised eight people to come to New York with her, but they bailed one by one for cost and other reasons. She has a sty on her left eye, which she seems mildly self-conscious of. A plate of eggs bread and fried potatoes, and another of French toast in syrup. Carbs carbs carbs, you get brain fog just looking at em. Working as a nursing assistant, studying to be an IC nurse. Her health insurance covered the diagnosis of her sty as non-malign, but not its removal. 'I even had to make a co-payment' – ie pay part from own pocket – 'for the diagnosis'. Her insurance will not allow her to be treated at the hospital where she works.

On FOX, Beck holds up book after book: *The Coming Insurrection*, by the Invisible Committee, a pamphlet by a group of French teenage techno-anarchists. A flyer for a tired Trotskyist conference in New York in November. Another euro anarchist book called *We Are An Image of the Future* is featured – I take a note to check that one on Amazon. Beck is now setting my reading list.

Taxi-driver in Newark: ex-Circuit City electronics store manager. In Seattle, ex Boeing engineer. In Orlando, ex-building contractor.

Billboard for anti-suicide campaign in Indiana: tomorrow will be better.

FOX News Channel, Redeye programme: a conservative commentator is asked what Obama will do should the GOP take the House. Well, he'll have to make a blackflip the guy says. The remark hangs in the air until a black conservative woman makes a joke about it. Everyone laughs nervously.

Colorado GOP Senate candidate on homosexuality: 'you can choose your partners. But birth has an influence, sure, as it does in conditions like homosexuality.'

New Jersey governor Craig Christie cancels the first Manhattan–New Jersey tunnel to be proposed for a century. Cost imbalances are a legit concern, yet the failure of the largest urban conglomerate in the world to connect itself is a measure of the failure of basic ambition. No matter. Ten new stories tomorrow will tell us of the unique dynamism of American life.

Beck: he has on a Wall Street guy who's written a book on the collapse of the global financial system, which he says will occur within a fortnight once it starts. His account is indistinguishable from eschatological Marxism-Leninism. Beck has put his timeline on a massive white board which stretches the length of the studio. Will this be a grand collapse, he asks the guest? Yes, but then something goes wrong. 'I believe it will be a time for the people of the world to come together to work together as one people.' This was not the answer solicited.

'We had a mouse.' Ad for a new mice-disposal unit, which lowers a whole canopy on the hapless rodent as it snaps its neck. Allows you to dispose of the body in the garbage without seeing it. The tagline: 'protect what's yours'. It would be sophomoric indeed to mention that Wikileaks released their 400,000 Iraq war documents cache today.

Civic voting campaign: Remember, even if you're not satisfied with the process, the important thing is to participate.

Guy selling a street newspaper in Columbus. 'Man, I'm a veteran. I'm ill.' Why can't he get Medicaid, benefits? 'Man I just got tired of the bureaucracy, making the submissions.' It is impossible to tell whether he has genuinely been wronged by institutions, or is mad. But a genuine universal care system would not oblige us to ask that question. He would simply be treated. He shows me a burn on his knuckles. Having gained an apartment, he went down to the riverside camp he used to live at, to help, and fell in a fire. Saint? Hopeless fuckup? I suspect he has a great talent for chaos. But that may be a way for me of moving on.

In Portland, Maine, a news story about a fundraiser for a local girl gone missing in New York. It is to be a spaghetti supper, with music by local DJ Demento. The girl was 'not afraid of anything' and was an escort working through Craigslist. Her family suspect people trafficking.

Down to the market briefly in Seattle, Pike's Place, to see the first ever Starbucks, opened in 1971. Now it looks like every other Starbucks. It would be crushingly disappointing if it did not.

I shudder for the day when Glenn Beck discovers the collected works of Bob Avakian. For he *is* Bob Avakian, the mirror, both of them predicting imminent doom for the entire system. When Beck does finally encounter him, he will meet the only man in the world more censorious of French anarchism than he. Avakian will become a regular commentator on Beck's show. This will happen before May 2011.

USA Network has a *House* marathon. To foreign viewers the appeal is that of a Sherlock Holmes in the medical world. To Americans, it is the bracing idea that a doctor could be effective without being empathetic, that what you are getting from healthcare is not cuddliness, that it does not matter whether the doctor is nice to you or not.

Supporters of Rand Paul stomp on the head of a protester from MoveOn, giving her concussion. Later, the man identified as doing the stomping appears on TV to demand an apology from the woman.

Bob Herbert in the NYT: American cities have century-old

sewage systems. What's going on? Americans should have water systems that are the envy of the world. Even a liberal columnist, talking offhand, cannot discuss issues without having to resort to exceptionalism. Yes, we're going to have the best damn sewage in the world.

What one thing could happen that would improve your life:
'That would be health insurance...'
'It would have to be health insurance...'
'I would need health insurance...'

Rupert Murdoch in the *Australian Financial Review*: he criticises Bill O'Reilly, for an 'easy' interview of Hillary Clinton, laying into the only commentator on FOX who has shown signs of rationality. This international corporate financier, however, loves Glenn Beck, who wants to return to the gold standard and would make the sort of financial arabesques that has made News Limited possible, impossible. 'He's a true libertarian. He's got millions of viewers...' He does indeed. Beck is raising an army against usury, against speculation. Murdoch thinks he can control these people. Thinks.

USA Today headline: 'Bridge over canyon triumph of American know-how.'

'Providence is next, next Providence, Providence in two minutes...'

9.

The Suburbs of Providence

**lincoln chafee and the rhode
island reds, thursday 28 october**

Before a broad semi-circular glass wall, the autumnal parkland of
Bryant University stretching off into the distance behind, the six men
running for governor were about to give their final summing up.
Night had fallen, and the campus was lit up, the flaming red, yellows,
browns bleeding through. The well-heeled audience wore League of
Women Voters buttons; smartly-dressed New Englanders, neat J-Crew
college kids. The six candidates arraigned across the stage, all men,
looked a little shifty and seedy, before all that nature. The moderator
turned to the guy at furthest left, Frank Algieri, bald and greyish, in a
black shirt. He was a pharmacist, but he had the appearance of an
accountant for the Mob. 'Now Mr Algieri it is time to begin your
summing up...' 'Well I would like to begin by spending some time on
the positive qualities of my opponents...'.

None of the other five looked particularly surprised by this feint.
Nor did any of the audience. Indeed, the entire debate had been
conducted with great politesse – even by the Democratic candidate
Frank Caprio, who had made national headlines days earlier by
telling President Obama to 'shove it', when he came to the state and
failed to endorse him. A sharp-faced little mutt of a man, Caprio kept
himself on a leash throughout, though you could see he was straining
at it. The debate ranged over the pros and cons of bond issues,
legalising prostitution and drugs, all talked about on a case-by-case

basis. The Republican candidate talked about a need to help the worst off. Everyone agreed that alternatives to prison should be promoted. I'd come to Rhode Island to see what a New England campaign was like. Now I knew. It was like Old England, or Europe at least. I had left New York mid afternoon, watched the grime and grey of Jersey give way to the burning riot of Fall, slept on the train, and woken up in Sweden.

The man I'd mainly come to see was Lincoln Chafee, the blonde-haired, slightly ethereal candidate at the right of the panel. Chafee had been a Senator for the state from 2000 to 2006, appointed to and then winning the office held by his father. He had never made much secret of his moderate credentials, voting with the Democrats far more often than the Republicans, and earning the title Number One RINO (Republican In Name Only). But even that was insufficiently liberal for Rhode Islanders, who replaced him with a Democrat in 2006. After that, he became head of Republicans and Independents for Obama, and barnstormed the country getting the vote out, both in the primaries and the election proper. Now he's running as an independent for Governor, hence Obama's withholding of an endorsement for the Democratic candidate. At this point in time, the prospect of finding a moderate Republican close to hand seemed remote, so I had come to America's smallest state, an island with a little hinterland, so that I could see at least what a lapsed Republican looked like.

To be honest, the answer is, a little flaky. Chafee's a slight man, even a touch delicate of feature, and surprisingly nervous, mucking up his syntax under the pressure of questioning, failing to make the hard-sell on his policies. How would you continue recovery in the state? 'Well, uh what we've done I mean look at the rail link we've made from the Amtrak to the airport, only airport in the country with Amtrak right in there, and we know from history that commerce grows around transport hubs goes back six thousand years from crossroads, uh river fords…' He had a beatific smile as he said put all this out there, for the audience to re-assemble with added parts of speech. His bunchy blondish hair had the effect of a halo. He had clearly done a lot of reading. James Taylor would play him in a made-for-TV movie; failing that, Chevy Chase, reprising his Clark Griswald role ('OK Rusty, we're going to build a transport hub'). Chafee's bio said that he'd spent a decade of his life as a farrier. That seemed to make sense as a New England hippie sort of thing, in the spirit of Ben and Jerry, two Vermont deadheads making an ice-cream empire. After the hippie-country-fayre thing, he went back into the family business, with the hope of building bridges and making things happen. It's possible that Lincoln Chafee was just a little too good for this world, let alone American politics. No matter how badly he stumbled, he never lost the twinkle in his eye.

Frank Caprio was determined to put it out, with a lit cigarette if necessary. A Rahm Emmanuel style old-skool ward-heeler candidate, he had a sharp-cut olive suit, and the air of a head bouncer going places. He had to knock Chafee off to win, and he didn't hold back.

'Yeah uh I would say it's gonna take a lot more than a train to really make this state happen. Dat's why you've got to have someone who knows what dere doin' in dis job...' The debate had commenced with the inevitable question for Caprio: why had he told the President of the United States, and the leader of his party, to 'shove it'? 'Look I respect Obama,' he said, shearing off the title and thus disrespecting him, 'but he can't come into this state and take away half a million in donations and not know how dis state is hurting, I gotta talk up for Rhode Island'. Translation: 'OK so dis brother's in the jump seat now, dat don't mean that Frankie Caprio's gonna just roll over and get screwed like a pooch know what I'm sayin'? We only just got the party off the goddam Irish, fuck alla youse if you think we're handing it over to the blacks.'

'Mr Chafee, would you like to respond to that using your wildcard?' Say what, now? Turns out I'd missed the very beginning of the debate, and it had rules. 'Now we're having a quickfire response round where no wild-cards may be used. However every unused wildcard can be counted for an extra thirty seconds of time in the final statements. If this had happened in Oklahoma, they would still be explaining the rules on election day. So on the one hand, designed on the assumption of an intelligence, on the other it resembles an episode of *Jeopardy* ('Frank?' 'Yeah can I have "go fuck yourself" for fiddy dollars thanks Regis?'). Community service and shove it, Europe and not-Europe. The double character of Rhode Island didn't resolve itself as I came back into Providence, a city vastly and recently built at its centre, with old red-brick mills meticulously restored, joined by textured, smartly finished knowledge-campus buildings. The Amtrak station was new, a handsome stone edifice, and the lacerating effect of a 70s-vintage four way flyover had been all but resolved. I imagined that the city centre would fill with people in open-necked shirts and slung laptops during the day, grabbing a coffee ahead of their meeting with other molecular biology software PhDs.

After some delay, Providence is taking up the high-tech overspill of Boston's Route 128. Various candidates in the governor's debate had banged on about the state's finances, and the parlous state thereof, but Providence didn't appear to be the worse for it. Lo and behold, something of the name had reshaped its spirit: Providence, unlike most elsewhere had had some investment put into it. The double-character thing came from the fact that I was being driven through it in a town-car with a blue unicorn on the side.

'Yeah, all dis shit went up a few years back.' Joey had picked me up the university after the debate, the vast cream sedan attracting glances amid the dark snub-nosed smart cars. The unicorn occupied the entire back panel of the car on the side. It was a demure beast, amid a landscape of tufted blue-white clouds, riding through the old row house streets. Three hundred pounds, in a coffee and brown two-tone shirt, Joey had a outline beard of such style and elegance that it gave poise to his great fat face. It thickened slightly at the goatee, thinned out to a line along the jaw, and then hooked over the ears, stopping just short of the scalp. It was quite possible that more work when into its design, execution and maintenance than into Obama's healthcare plan. Joey punched the radio button until we hit the opening chords of 'Take My Breath Away', and we turned sharply into Federal Hill.

'Yeah, dere's two Rhode Islands. Diss is mine.' Down the main drag to De Pasquale Plaza, I could see what he meant. To anyone whose mental image of the state is limited to Newport, and losing a yacht race to the Americans every four years, Rhode Island could be mistaken for a large country club, run for the white ducks set. But what I was looking at was little Calabria. It was an old wooden district that the protestants had long vacated. In their stead was a series of trattoria, upmarket pizzerias, and downmarket bars, full of dark-haired women named Maria chewing out hapless Match.Com dates: 'Honey let me tell you when a man goes out with me when a man goes out with me I expect a standard you know I expect a standard. And what you are wearing is not a standard. It is not. Hey Rita gimme another limoncello'.

I had heard that Rhode Island was the only majority Catholic state in the country, and assumed that that was made up of Boston Irish overspill. So to a degree it is, but it is also the farther shore of Naples. Though federally the state is one of the most Democratic in the nation, the Italians have supplied their fair share of moderate Republicans who helped give the place its current, sane, demeanour. These include the current governor Donald Carcieri, and the longtime 'supermayor' of Providence, Vincent 'Buddy' Cianci, who ran the city for twenty years, in two bursts. Like Chafee, Cianci eventually left the GOP to become an independent. It was during his second go at City Hall in the 1980s that the place was regenerated – at the same time as many US cities were putting themselves beyond recovery. The city turned its old mills into malls and hotels, rebuilt the train station, and redeveloped the river, which had been covered by expressways in the 50s. True, Cianci would later run into some, erm, bother – he would eventually serve four years for corruption, a move in US city politics roughly comparable to taking a post-electoral fellowship at the Brookings Institute. But the state seems to have come out of it a lot better than others, the product of a shared mildly pragmatic politics.

The reconditioned mills tell their own story, of a state remaking itself rather than living off past glory or luxuriating in the tsunami of bullshit passing currently passing for a debate on national direction.

What was most notable about the governors' debate was that there was not a single mention from any candidate, of exceptionalism, or 'we're Americans, our trousers are the envy of the world'. Not any of that. People just talked about the issues. Frank Caprio – Obama's sternest critic in the debate – mentioned the recent Rhode Island floods, 'worst in our country's history, worse than Katrina'. But you didn't hear about them, because they handled it, in an efficient and orderly fashion.

Back at the hotel – an all-white extravaganza, white tiles, white sofa, white misty cotton bedspread, as if the whole thing had been executed to the personal design of Marisa Tomei, I watched Jon Stewart's interview with Obama, which occupied his entire half-hour show. The President's decision to appear on a satire/comedy show had attracted much criticism from the likes of CNN among others – which would be fine if CNN had not long ago abandoned the most basic practice of critical inquiry into the news it relays, leaving the field to people like Stewart. The Obama interview was softball in places – though nothing compared to the North Korean style of FOX news dealing with Sarah Palin, *inter alia* – but it managed to get to the nub of Obama's problem, in selling the torturous process of reform:

Stewart: With health care and these health exchanges not kicking in until 2014, the question is, can we still say 'yes, we can?'
Obama: Yes, we can...
Stewart: Mmmmm...
Obama: But...
(studio laughter, some groans)

On the other news channels, they were still running with the Rand Paul incident, in which a half-dozen of the Tea Party Kentucky Senate candidate's supporters had lammed on a MoveOn supporter, pushing her to the ground, and putting a boot on her neck. The man in question, a Paultard hipster type named, of course, Terry Prophet, would later appear on television to fie his side of the story. Bizarrely he would only allow himself to be shown below the neck, even though his image was everywhere. Faced with widespread condemnation, he went on the attack and claimed that the woman should apologise to him. His reasons for using his boot were perfectly legitimate, he insisted – 'I have some issues with my back'. That appeared to be the capper really, the perfect expression of right-wing squaddist politics, American-style, a mixture of equal parts brutality, self-pitying victimhood and inadequate health care.

Both major American political parties are really mega-parties containing utterly different and opposed groups, and have been for decades, for more than a century. Even so, the moderate Republicans, pragmatic country-club types and Tea Partiers stretch the notion of a coalition to the breaking point. 'The big story isn't the problems of the Democrats,' the journalist and former Clinton advisor Sidney Blumenthal says. 'The big story is the coming civil war in the Republican party. None of these guys like each other. It's political and personal. Everyone hates John Boehner, for example. There's no insurgency. The Tea Party is just the hard right of the Republican Party, nothing else. This is a civil war.'

You would think this is something that the Obama team would be able to take advantage of. You would think. But even faced with the dark gift of the Rand Paul stomping, the moment that might detach or dissuade a section of wavering Tea Party sympathisers from its crazy base, there was no one among the Democrats who could or would sheet it home. Surely at this point, Barack Obama could have brought himself closer to the American centre, by expressing an anger and outrage, we're American, this doesn't happen here, and so on? The Right have just spent the last three days banging on about the sacking of Juan Williams, an NPR (public radio) commentator who appears as a semi-liberal shil on FOX News, after some inadvised oversharing about being made nervous by Muslims at airports. 'What's on Mr Williams' mind is between he and his psychiatrist,' NPR's head had said, announcing his dismissal, an epitome of liberal blundering, which the Right turned into an attack on public-funded media. It's a measure of the Democrats' classic loss of politically speaking, all self-belief, that they managed to underplay actual violence.

***

The next day, on the train back to New York, the *Times* had further instalments on the voting groups that the Democrats have shed, and failed to regain. In the *New York Times*, David Leonhardt has an article detailing the failure of the White House to stay on the gas pedal after some false, signs of job recovery appeared at the end of 2009. You can't blame people for abandoning the party that has abandoned them, but an accompanying piece gives no clarity as to what people want. In Ohio, people are angry at 'the debt', 'the bailout', and even at the proposal to end tax breaks for those earning $250,000+ per annum.

Never blame the people for your own political failure, the old adage goes, but American voters test that moral to the very limit. Voter after voter who are going to try the Republicans, because they are angered by the 'change that's come out of far left field' – as if Obama had not made his commitment to a comprehensive healthcare plan, a new energy jobs creation plan, and many more big ticket items amply clear. Now, they were going to try something else, even if it be the exact opposite. The Obama administration failed them, but many of them, in terms of what they want, should be going left, not right. But there is no place to go. The US is no Rhode Island. The Republican right taking over, the people that many Rhode Island Republicans couldn't stay in a party with, will take office, their hand on the Bible, with a copy of *Atlas Shrugged* beneath.

I was thinking all this, papers spread out in the train's club car, when there was a whoomp, and a sound like something full being hit hard, the train slowed and stopped, and the desk light went off. The conductors lounging near the cafebar suddenly looked pale, their walkie talkies crackled and they headed towards the back. When they came back they were hearty again, relieved. 'We hit a deer,' one said. It was clear what they had first believed we had hit. I realised that I'd heard it happen. It was that whoomp, a sort of liquid bang, something emptying out. But everyone was relieved. Nothing terrible had happened, we'd just killed Bambi. After ten minutes, the lights came back on, we started up, and continued towards New York.

10.

This is a Sign About Nothing

the rally for sanity, washington dc
saturday 30 october

By the last Saturday in October, and the final news cycles of the election, it had become clear that the Democrats would not make up the shortfall, and were heading for an electoral disaster. Two weeks earlier, the polls had stood at a 6% advantage to the Republicans; by some measure they were now at 8%. The barnstorming campaign of Barack Obama, Michelle, Joe Biden and Bill Clinton had had little measurable effect. The message that change was coming slowly and was difficult had not resonated, nor had the idea that voting the GOP back in would be handing the keys back to the people 'who had driven the car into the ditch in the first place'. The various antics of Tea Party Republicans had not dimmed the public enthusiasm for a change – but nor more tellingly had the repeated refusal by Republican candidates to specify exactly what programmes they would cut to achieve deficit reduction. Candidate after candidate came on the news channels, and grimly held the age-old line – we'll find savings, efficiencies, eliminate waste and duplication. But we won't cut Medicare or defence, or border protection or veterans entitlements.

If this non-sequitur was causing any disquiet for the electorate, they didn't show it. The swing to the Republicans was made up equally of conservatives who stayed away in '08 coming back, Democrats sitting '10 out, and an equal parts swing vote/anti-political vote by independents. One poll showed that 25% of voters wanted to sack everyone and start again, a reaction equal parts acute rejection of the political class, and fantasy of some pre-political innocence that could somehow be regained.

The problem for the Democrats was not that the public was speaking with one voice, but that there was no prevailing counter-trend in their favour, by any group. Since 2008, they had squandered the advantage they held with a pluralist base, treating the business of politics with lofty arrogance, borne of life in a lawyerly and technocratic bubble. Nothing could explain this except profound isolation brought about in part by the furious rate of bill-making they had undertaken – an isolation which magnified and made disastrous Barack Obama's worst political defect, a deep unwillingness to go toe-to-toe with opponents in any sort of deliberate, disciplined or strategic fashion when it was absolutely required. That it was the reverse side of one of his great political skills – the capacity to effectively take and command the high ground at crucial moments – only made it all the more damnable that he could not find the capacity to switch into an alien mode when it became absolutely necessary. The only thing more disconcerting than the Obama administration's failure to acknowledge political shortcomings, was what they said when they did. According to Maureen Dowd, a senior aide to Obama had stated that 'the President was beginning to realise that he had not used his charm effectively' in selling his policies. Oy vey. Until the final week of the campaign, it had been possible to believe that something, anything might make it possible for the Democrats to narrow the gap. By the final weekend, all chance of this was gone – what hope there was resided, as usual, in the possibility that the polls might be off.

Such final weekends are usually bitter occasions, but America's liberals had something to cheer and distract them this time around: the *Daily Show* host Jon Stewart's 'Rally For Sanity', something he had announced and spruiked for weeks past on his 11pm show. The rally had been 'combined' with a sham alternative rally – 'to increase fear' – by Stephen Colbert, whose FAUX news style programme *The Colbert Report* back-ends Stewart's show. Two weeks prior to the rally, Colbert announced that he had failed to get a permit, and the event became a rally for sanity and/or fear, the poster a loose takeoff of the famous blue and red Obama 'hope' image, showing Stewart and Colbert as a two-header monster out of 50s sci-fi. Stewart had conceived of the rally following Glenn Beck's quasi-hysterical 'Restoring Honour' rally, held at the Washington Mall on August 28, the 47th anniversary of Martin Luther King's 'March on Washington' at the same place. It was intended to be a focused response to the hyperbole of much right-wing protest occurring since Obama's inauguration – Stewart was said to be particularly disturbed by the tendency of some Tea Partiers to compare Obama to Hitler, and the proliferation of Hitler moustaches as a poster-motif. With the megaphone of his late night TV show, Stewart began building the rally as an event in September, and setting the tone – that of an appeal to moderation, reciprocity and mutual good faith, in place of the obsessive divisionalism of the various right-wing movements. This included a 'try out your sign' online feature, where people could post ideas for their signs and test their 'level of sanity' (a Tea Party style poster overflowing with words about one 'one world government' etc was counterposed with a simple placard reading 'got competence'?). Stewart would later say that he had worried, on the eve, about the size of the rally. But it had been clear from Facebook sign-ups and the like that it was going to be a major event. By eight in the morning, the streets were already choked with people making their way from Union Station to the Mall. They were every sort of age, and all pretty much down at heel, sweats and cheap tops, jeans and faded t-shirts, hipsters of all ages, together with more lumpenish satire consumers in chinos, check shirts and non-matching windbreakers.

A few costumes, four guys dressed like bananas, Paris Hiltons and Sarah Palins, generic Halloween schlock, the occasional tricorn hat. And signs, lots of signs. 'Somewhat Irritated About Extreme Outrage', 'This is the first sign of the apocalypse', 'I hope this isn't a trap', 'Got sanity?' 'Restore sanity, legalise pot', 'What do we want?' 'Moderation when in a reasonable time frame', and so on. Some pro-printed, painstakingly lettered, others handwritten on card. There was a fair degree of self-referentiality: 'This is a sign', 'My arms are tired' 'I wish I hadn't brought this' and so on.

By nine, the Mall was full two blocks deep. By ten, a hundred thousand had showed up. *Daily Show* clips were pumping out of the screens, friends were meting up and comparing costumes, deaf signers were relaying everything from a small stage in the middle. By noon, there were a hundred and fifty thousand, stretching all the way back along the grass, spilling into the side streets. A *Daily Show* clip faded out mid-gag, an announcement: 'ladies and gentlemen, the Roots!' and we kicked off with a bass throb and a forcing beat. The Rally To Restore Sanity had started.

It was exciting, it was wild, it was a mad carnival – and, it has to be said, something of a fizzer. It was all a little bit nothing, a little bit meh, it was something that had to be great to be good, and was just all right. It was odd and underdone and half-assed. It was a perfect expression of American progressivism today.

Stewart had emerged about fifteen minutes in, after music from said Roots, and John Legend, and a bit of schtick from the *Mythbusters* team. 'Thank you thank you for coming' he said, sounding more relieved than welcome, like a nervous party host. Halfway into that, Stephen Colbert appeared on screen, ostensibly in a bunker below – the first instalment on the hope vs fear thing. It was the routine they would rely on throughout – the interruption thing, flogged to death.

They did it in the next act, when Cat Stevens/Yusuf Islam came out to sing 'Peace Train' – sigh of recognition and an ooooh of pleasure from the woodstockier sections of the crowd – only to be interrupted by Ozzy Osborne singing ... something, signifying ... something. By this time, anyone who had entertained vague doubts about the focus and impact of a rally not to rally, was feeling that they had been more than confirmed. As a sort of loose, funky, fun gathering, the rally was all right. People seemed to be enjoying it. But three quarters of an hour in, it was growing to no point, lacking momentum, or a sense of gathering force. After the musical stars schtick, Stewart and Colbert gave out awards for reasonableness – a baseball player who didn't curse out an umpire for making a wrong call, the woman who stood up and told Obama 'I'm tired of defending you' (she did it reasonably), and so on. There was a serious song from Kid Rock (!) and Sheryl Crow, and then a comedy song from Stewart and Colbert about the things that unite us being more important than etc etc, called 'The Greatest Strongest Country In The World' and then a pretty funny montage of fear-mongering. And once again, it was nice, but by now the rally felt like it hadn't actually ever started, that the whole thing was its own warm-up.

Clearly, the organisers had decided early on that there would be no lecturing, no worthiness or plain seriousness. The question was, for godsakes, why not? If there was ever a bookish, ideas-oriented mass crowd in recent American history this was it. For two years they have been led by one of the most educated and intellectual Presidents in recent American history, and one who has done everything to obscure that part of his being. Filling the vacuum has been the mystical fidelism of the Tea Party and its supporters, elevating the Constitution from the status of founding document, to that of being a total expression of government, not merely the first word concerning the relation between a state and its people, but the last one as well. This simplistic message has become a wellspring of energy for the Right, because It gives an effective story, a myth of the Fall, which complements their sense of dislocation. That the Republicans honour this fidelism wholly in the breach and none in the observance is of no importance; the message is intended to give a sense of meaning, order and purpose to a chaotic and sprawling society.

Progressives are good at criticising this mythologisation of modern life, but for decades they have been without a counter-argument, and simple and widely understood view of human life and America that could be marshalled against the Right. That is why the man leading this rally is a TV satirist, and the rally he is leading has, at its heart, satire's absence. Could the organisers not have found someone to enunciate an idea not merely of reasonableness, but of reason, and its virtues, and how that refutes any notion that good government and the good life can be guaranteed by a 1787 pamphlet you can slip into your back pocket? The answer is no, and that goes to the heart of the dilemma for American liberals. For the founding compact of modern American liberalism was laid down by FDR in his 1941 'State of the Union' address, in his notion of the 'four freedoms': freedom of speech and expression, freedom of worship, freedom from want, freedom from fear.

This quartet became so much a part of American self-conception during the period of the mid-twentieth century that they were illustrated by Norman Rockwell. Yet a moment's inspection makes clear that they are a substantial revision of American notions of freedom, the latter two being positive freedoms, enabling the material possibility of being autonomous human beings, drawn from the tradition of European social philosophy, rather than the negative freedoms from the rationalist English tradition which underpins the American founding. It underpins the distinctive double of social progressivism and economic social democracy (or the remnants of it) that constitutes American liberalism, yet it remains unspoken. It is undoubtedly the implicit belief of a man like Stewart, and the vast majority of the people attending the rally – and beneath it is the belief that a present people does not live in fealty to an ancient document, but creates its own life in each present moment. Why is the there no one to step up and say these things? Why when a comedian feels that he has no alternative but to step up and say these things, cannot he find people to say them? Can he say them himself?

We were about to find out, as Stewart announced that he was about to say something serious. But first we had to last through a long schtick whereby Colbert kept interrupting him, with the help of a giant puppet version of himself. And finally Stewart made the speech proper, and there were times when it teetered on being an anti-speech: 'just by you being here that is the most important thing that has happened today...' he began. The thing teetered on the edge of falling over altogether.

He had a point when he got going. Sadly, it wasn't that much of one. Zeroing in on the new intolerance, he put the blame squarely on the media and punditry and the '24-hour conflictinator of cable news'. 'People are always telling us "we can't work together to get things done, but the truth is we do. We work together to get things done every damn day. The only place we don't is here or on cable TV. We live in hard times, not end times...the media is our magnifying glass – they can hold it up to society, or they can use it to burn ants.'

Finally, he flashed live overhead footage of cars trying to get into the DC traffic tunnel, three lanes squeezing down to two: 'see everyone in those cars has their own individual truth – atheist Republican computer programmer, gay Mormon creationist...' etc, but 'that doesn't matter here they just take it in turns: "you go then I'll go"'... before tailing off into near apology for holding the rally at all, and a musical finale. Even that was non-committal: 'I'll take you there'. Where? And then we left. 'What did you think?' 'Ah, it was all right.' Vaguely disconsolate, trudging back along Connecticut Avenue, I tried to work out in my head where I thought it had all gone wrong. By the time we made Union Station, besieged by geeks and hipsters, like ants round a sugar cube, it seemed to me that it was a question not merely of execution but of basic design and intent.

After all, there's nothing wrong with holding a rally for reason, nor more moderation, but when you suggest that the latter is served by accepting everyone's world view as valid, then you betray the former. It's one thing to decry the use of Hitler moustaches on anyone you dislike, but if by that token you then accept the reasonably phrased notion that Barack Obama is a socialist, that global warming is a plot, or that a 21st century state can be run entirely on the basis of the Constitution, then you've given the game away – and been more than a little disingenuous. The tirades of Glenn Beck, Rush Limbaugh and the like are not merely both extreme and uncivil, they are uncivil because their extremism is in error, and thus finds no purchase in reality. There's nothing wrong with extremism per se, for under any such rubric can be included everyone from Gandhi to Mandela and all points between and beyond. But it's the reason underlying such extremism that gives it such grace – and it is grace that is so conspicuously lacking in the flecked violence of speech and deed directed against Obama, and anything remotely progressive in America today.

Currently, the news doing the rounds is the report by the NAACP digging into the racist and supremacist associations of some key Tea Party figures – especially those associated with a couple of 'peak' groups, 1776 Tea Party, and Resist Net. NAACP's report uncovers an extensive interconnection between old minuteman and militias networks, and some (though not all) of the Tea Party groups. This is the recrudescence of the constitutionalist fidelism, and the other source of its energy. It is the implicit existence of the Constitution and the revolutionary founding, as a white *ethnos*, the myth binding together a particular people – Anglo-Celtic descended white Americans. Others can enjoy, but only as a marginal presence. This nativism is not the whole of the Tea Party, but it is much of it, and Stewart's idea that all 'extremism' is somehow equivalent, gives continued cover to the most atavistic Americanist ideas emerging from within the Tea Party.

Some things can't be solved by asking everyone to play nice. At some point, if you're going to draw a quarter of a million or so – six billion in Stephen Colbert's estimate – to hear what you have to say, you better stand up and say that while there are many ways to look at a thing, some of them are plain wrong, and pernicious in their error.

Can American liberalism, or whatever succeeds it, be regrounded? Not in its prior form. The intellectual fusion of social progressivism and economic social democracy itself relied on a class alliance, between one section of middle-class professionals and the organised working class. The latter are now so scattered, and their basic agenda so betrayed by the Democrats – a party almost wholly dominated by progressivist professionals – that the alliance has been sundered. Many of the working class now feel they may as well take their chances with whatever the Republicans can do, because they –

through the good offices of the Tea Party – appear to be the group with a firm idea of the way forward. Why not give them a go? It can't hurt, so the thinking goes. Because there is no alternative story, no countermyth to lead a people out of the valley of the shadow.

Absent of anything more sophisticated, the Tea Party's constitutional fidelism *becomes* an expression of reason, because it is an actual philosophical account of reality. An eighteenth-century account, but an account nevertheless. What the march for sanity offered was the idea that civility must implicitly be passionless, that it necessarily involves someone else going first – and hence the acknowledgement of their equal right. I go, then you go. For many at the Mall, living and working in a world of complex systems and relativities, nothing could be more reflective of their idea of social life than 'I go, then you go.' But that, by definition, cannot be mapped onto politics when what is at stake is the shaping of a programme and the reshaping of social reality. And so their suggestibility, their malleability, their persuadability is the means by which no strong programme can be enunciated.

It may be nearly terminal. Coming back from the rally towards Union Station, we stopped off at one of the two Irish bars nestled opposite the old Post Office. Space was at a premium, so everyone was jammed up together. There was a nice young couple from Minnesota there. What did they think of the rally? 'It was uh good, it was kinda neat.' What did we think? 'It was shit,' my girlfriend said, outlining its shortcomings, its evasive easiness and failure to take a stand. They thought for a second. Then said: 'Yeah, I guess you're right.'

11.

The Tea Party Express Rolls Home

monday, 1 november

The gold dome of the New Hampshire statehouse was shining in the dark when the Tea Party Express rolled down Main Street Concord tonight. Whoever organised the end of this tour knew what they were doing – unsurprisingly, as this grassroots movement is attended at every stage by well-paid professional consultants. Yeah and verily, the dome was like a beacon unto freedom, the main street was prosperous and well-ordered, and the granite-staters gathered in the statehouse garden looked hardy and appropriately resilient. There were about three hundred of them, chunky locals, mildly amused at the out-of-town reporters freezing their bajinkos off in the chill New England air. There was the usual redwhiteandbluiana, the same stalls – the Constitution explained, 'Tales of Heroes in Iraq', weirder conspiratorial tracts, ceremonial lanterns (Paul Revere), and of course the yellow 'Don't Tread On Me' flag, with its coiled snake below. And the same people leading it off, the plain grassroots folks with suspiciously slick public speaking skills, coming off the bus: 'y'all put on a good showing New Hampshire!' Cheers. 'Who loves our Constitution?' More cheers.

Another day, another Tea Party? This one is the Tea Party Express, an outfit separate to the Tea Party Patriots, and with whom they are engaged in a vicious war. Both are themselves umbrella groups for the thousands of Tea Party organisations that have sprung up in the last two years. As these midterm elections enter their final twenty-four hours, the Tea Parties are their great moment before the gold dome. Whatever happens tomorrow, and afterward, and however it's been done, they've set the agenda for the election. No, not agenda. They've set the mood, temperature, background, mise en scene. Their sense of certainty and identity is unwavering, set in granite, while that of liberals and progressives comes and goes like a nimbus. Tonight's rally starts with the usual rah-rah, why are we here, because we're taking our country back, I'm taking my country back how bout you.'

This is Amy Kremer, appearing everywhere, the former air hostess from Atlanta, Georgia, a large woman who became politically active after quitting work for health reasons and, as she told Ed Pilkington of the *Guardian*, 'becoming tremendously depressed...I needed to fill a void.' Eighteen months after pulling together a proto-Tea Party on Twitter – and more than a year after it acquired the professional political leadership of Sal Russo, ex-Reagan hack, she's still leading it. Political training and rally flying hours have polished her to a fine sheen – she can get a crowd roaring, with one quick punch after the other. 'We can't spend our way out of debt – it's not rocket science!' Cheer. 'Harry Reid is our number-one target. After tomorrow we'll have another number-one target.' Cheer.

Rollicking stuff, but Kremer is just the taster. She's followed by Debbie Lee – 'mother of the first NavySEAL to be killed in Iraq!'. Cheer, of sorts. Debbie's got the chain store clothes and blonde girl-mullet hair, a sing-songy voice – and, it becomes clear, not a whit of shame about enrolling her dead son in a political campaign. She starts, as usual, thanking vets here for their service, our freedoms etc, and then segues into the story of how her son died. Behind her, another son is holding up a large poster photo of her dead boy Mark, turning it in a slow semi-circle so all the crowd can see.

'He was carrying the unit heavy gun...he stood up to give covering fire while his buddy was put in a medivac 'copter. When they all came back to base, he was asked to go out again. He didn't hesitate...'

On and on it goes, as her lilt becomes stagey and overdramatised, as if the material needed a little punching up. The emotions fight it out. It's a story of a brave and selfless death, being told with all the honesty of a Franklin Mint voice-over. 'He did this for us, for all of us, as many other have done, for our freedoms.' But of course he didn't, even if he thought he did. He died a meaningless death, thrown away on lies and political arse-covering. Does Debbie's way of telling it – that poster lifts almost out of the boy's hands, seems to float in the night air – recuperate meaning from grief? Maybe, but she doesn't give any indication that she ever doubted that it was meaningful – or that there would be nothing wrong in speaking of it beside a poster that said 'Flat Tax Now', enrolling her son's extinction in one side of a debate on fiscal policy.

After that, a short wiry woman, Diana Nagy, gives a spiel that effectively enrols every dead soldier in the Tea Party movement – 'my grandparents went to the Pacific and prayed over their dead brother's ocean grave knowing that this sort of thing is what we are fighting for!' Cheers. She finishes with a song 'my mom and I wrote' – 'Where Freedom Flies'. Nother rah-rah speech then Lloyd Marcus, a black, slightly fruity guy in leather comes out. 'Wooooooooooooh I'm not an African-American! I'm an American!' Cheers.

On it went and so could we, if we chose, marvelling at this exuberant movement, supercharged with secret money, but drawing on a substantial reserve of real energy, and strong ideas. The rally had a gleeful air about 'firing Pelosi' and 'giving Harry Reid his pink slip' (ie termination notice) 'and I'm going to go to the lingerie store to do it' said one woman, some bizarre twist on the 'man up Harry Reid' charge fired at him earlier by Sharron Angle (slip/slip, ysee, I guess). One presumes. What else could it be? Cheers, anyway. They probably will succeed in doing this. But they were also similarly triumphant about sacking Barney Frank, the liberal congressional headkicker from Massachusetts, and there's no chance that will happen, and so one wonders at what base level of rationality these people are thinking.

Innumerable polls have been trumpeting, with results suggesting that thirty forty fifty per cent of people support 'some of' the Tea Party's aims. But since these aims include things like 'strong national defence' and 'balanced budgets', the numbers are obviously inflated. A more realistic assessment is that no more than 2% of the country is involved or actively supportive of the Tea Party, to greatly varying degrees of commitment.

Beyond all the hoopla, there's a rational core to the Tea Party, which demands respect by Democrats – if for no other reason than that they cannot be adequately contested without understanding what piece of reality they have turfed up that no one else has. In Orlando, at the Palin rally, I'd scarfed around for the usual loonie vox pops, but finally approached a middle-aged woman dressed, well, less flagrantly madly, than the other participants. So I'd asked her one of the usual healthcare questions. Given that the so-called Obamacare is really Romneycare, as pioneered in Massachusetts, I'd asked, why the sudden horror? Well, she said I really don't have a problem with it, per se, if it's levied at the state level. It's unconstitutional at the federal level. And if the Supreme Court ruled that it was, in fact, constitutional? She thought for a second, looked troubled, and then said: well I would have to think hard about that.

What was so interesting was not so much her faith in the torturous process by which policy had to be drip filtered through the country's archaic political system, as the degree of disjuncture that the possible constitutionality of Obamacare had created in her. She took no recourse in the usual rodomontade about liberal judges. She deferred to the separation of powers. She simply couldn't believe that Obama's health care plan would ever be ratified. It stopped her in her tracks.

More to the point, in Seattle, I'd spoken to Keli Carender, a blogger and educationist who writes under the name of 'Liberty Belle' – and like many right-wing women, not all of them on FOX news, has a certain trade in exhibitionism, posing on her blog as Supergirl in what appears to be body paint, but is in fact a skin-tight costume. Carender is often spoken of as one of the two or three 'founders' of the Tea Party movement. Several weeks after Obama's inauguration, she started a 'porkulus' protest against unnecessary spending. The protest fielded several hundred people from a few internet postings, and she was off. The Tea Party movement 'came from people like me who thought you could just vote and go home and that we didn't have to keep an ever-watchful eye on the politicians'.

'We generally trusted the political class, even those with whom we disagreed. Well, we finally realized that the citizenry must constantly be guarding against the self interest of the politicians...I used to consider myself a Republican and I think many of were lulled into thinking that Bush was doing okay because he was "our guy". We learned that lesson the hard way that that just isn't necessarily true, and unfortunately I think Obama supporters are also going to have to learn that lesson.' She's one of the Tea Partiers who see the movement as distinct from the Republican party, and potentially, eventually, in opposition to it.

'The political class doesn't get it at all. They think this is all about electing Republicans and that we will just go home once that happens on November 2. But this not about Republicans at all, and if the Republicans get control of Congress and continue down the same path of overspending and backroom deals, then we will be there to throw them out in two years.'

Well, maybe. But there's grassroots and grassroots. After all, the idea of 'porkulus' protests was floated on, of all places, Rush Limbaugh's radio programme – and Carender's version of it gained wider publicity when it was relayed on the blog of ultra-right commentator Michelle Malkin. After that, Carender was whisked to DC for training with Dick Armey's FreedomWorks, and set back out. That is not to argue that she does not have a consistent set of beliefs, or would be an activist in her own cause. But it is to suggest that the vast network of conservative groups and the thinktanks have a capacity to take someone from zero to wherever in no time flat.

Perhaps that explains Christine O'Donnell, the Delaware candidate, popular enough to get the nomination, now fifteen points down against an opponent who once described himself (in jest) as a 'bearded marxist'. O'Donnell has made the news again by revealing that she does not know the contents of the first amendment, or indeed any of the others. 'Where in the first amendment is there a separation between church and state?' she said in a debate at a law school, the wide laughter suggesting she may have taken the know-nothing act too far. Or has she?

For anyone wanting to take the Tea Party as no more than a combination of performance art and abnormal psychology, Christine's your gal. The bubbly slightly kooky Jersey gal, latterly transformed into a Sarah Palin Gucci-knockoff made her way through the state primary for Republican candidate to contest Biden's vacated seat, with the help of a small but committed group of insurgents and out-of-state supporters, out of the various and rapidly pullulating groups on the right side of the net.

She appeared to come from nowhere, but it was in fact her third try. Indeed, she'd actually been the Republican candidate for the Senate in 2006 – simply because no one else was willing to go up against Biden, a god in the state, for reasons fair and foul. By that time, she had had several lifetimes. As would later become well-known, she was a soundbite pundit on Bill Maher's *Politically Incorrect* late-night show, a place with a constant demand for right-wingers who can play up and play the game. It was there she revealed, in that peekaboo way, that she had dabbled in witchcraft, and 'had a date on a satanic altar' – and hell, what gal bored like hell in Jersey hasn't? She went on to a start a degree in acting from an old Jersey liberal arts college rechristened as a university. She would later claim to have attended Oxford, after doing a week-long training course in the town of Oxford, not to mention a fraudulent claim to the distinguished Claremont University. And Princeton.

But when she quit the one actual degree she did do, it was after a religious-political revelation on seeing high-res abortion pix. Born a Catholic, she became a fundamentalist, before returning to Catholicism, and then saying she follows both. She became part of the rich Republican undergrowth, in California and transferred to Delaware when she took a job with the ultra-conservative Intercollegiate Studies Institute, which formally states that men should have precedence and authority over women. She then took the Institute to court for discriminating against her as a woman, had her house repossessed, and entered a decade of running in primaries and living off the public funds accruing from it. She believes masturbation is adultery, that Darwinism is a myth, and believes that the families of pregnant women who may die in childbirth should choose whether to save the child's life through birth or the mother's through abortion. She practiced abstinence in her 20s, though she was appearing on the MTV series *Sex in the 90s* at the time.

She is, in other words, a true product of the culture, of the maze of placeless suburbs, basic cable and outlet malls that the states of her birth now live beneath. She never completed the acting course, because she is still in it, taking on the shape of whoever last crossed her path. She is the last of small-town Americana drip-fed through eighties californication. She is what Robert Hughes, speaking of Andy Warhol's Factory-era retinue once called 'floating space debris'.

As such, she is both an embarrassment to the Tea Party, and its utter essence, people floating around in nowheresville, wondering where their country went, and their purpose with it, and finding it in notions of exceptionalism and providence. The mood is catching, an exuberance in the TP-ers touching on the manic. In Reno last Monday week, launching this express, Sarah Palin turned her hard-bop poetry-slam speechifying onto the Republican establishment 'well if the GOP doesn't get it, it'll be goodbye GOP.' Alaskan Tea Partier Joe Miller had his private security detail – consisting of moonlighting serving soldiers – handcuff a persistent journalist, after having given a speech in which he praised East Germany as a model of border protection. Glenn Beck urges his viewers to maintain their physical fitness, so that they will be better able to deal with the coming debt-based collapse of the United States and then the entire world. The Iowa Republican party asserts as the first plank of its manifesto that it believes in, and I quote 'life, liberty and the right to property (pursuit of happiness)', thus rewriting the document from which they claim foundation and meaning, just as FOX news tries to deny the separation of church and state.

But it is O'Donnell who has reached a state of know-nothingism that can only be described as homeopathic – through dilution, no trace of an idea remains, only the impression it left, just as she is nothing other than the impression others have left on her. Watching the grainy footage on TV is a wonder to behold. She returns to the topic, over and over, giving Coons no alternative but to speak to her like a dull student:

O'Donnell: Let me just clarify: You're telling me that the separation of church and state is found in the First Amendment?

Coons: Government shall make no establishment of religion...

O'Donnell: That's in the First Amendment...?

This is either guile beyond measure, forcing the wonkish, bookish Coons to talk all teacherly, or it is simple absence, a sign that she is nothing more than a serial public-funding grifter, and a terminal attention whore (to quote Diablo Cody's self-description). Her mother is on the payroll, she's charged shopping sprees to the public purse, and left campaigns hanging with unpaid wages and tens of thousands in debt. Like Sarah Palin's embarrassing snowbilly family, she has mistaken the party primary process for audience selection on *The Price is Right*. Others may win for any number of reasons. If O'Donnell does it can safely be assumed that Americans have abandoned any notion that they should choose a candidate who must actually act in the world, based on reflection, and have chosen instead a mere image of an image.

Indeed, though the Republicans will most likely take the House, and knock off Reid and other high profile senators like Russ Feingold, Wednesday will most likely see some right-wing soul searching, as it becomes clear that they've allowed the Democrats to retain control of the Senate. The Delaware vacancy that could have been taken by Republican Mike Castle will return to the Democrats, Alaska will go either to newly-minted independent Lisa Murkowski or even the hapless Democrat Scott McAdam, and the GOP may even fall short in Colorado and – though this is a long shot – Nevada. Such a result would create a comprehensive gridlock in politics, but also make it impossible for a two-house Republican congress to launch a full war against Obama – a war which will in any case include inquiries, subpoenas and everything all the way to attempts at impeachment. It will allow Obama, should he find the skills to do it, to run against the House – 'they're the ones screwing up the recovery' – and use the

Senate to protect existing legislation. The Tea Party will be left with the knowledge that they have given Obama a reprieve – and will also be tasked with trying to control a group of politicians who will have no choice but to play the political game, to get things done- compromise, earmarks, negotiation, all the bad things. Having drawn on their energy, the Republican Party is now trying to dismantle them, with Karl Rove being openly contemptuous – and he and others fearful that they may somehow get Sarah Palin nominated, a woman whom the Republicans believe will deliver them the sort of results gained by Goldwater and McGovern in decades past, a collapse to the base 35% of support, a disaster.

Beneath the floodlit gold dome, this party has an expectant air – but it may be something that many Tea Partiers, these ageing Reagan revolutionaries, back here in their 60s and 70s to get the feel once again of morning in America, look back on as the high point, the shining apex before the fall. Yet at the same time who could deny that theirs is the party of the stronger part, that the energy and hope is with them? Who could deny that especially after Saturday's 'Sanity' rally, that ultimate confession of liberal self-doubt, effacement, exhaustion of ideas and purpose? Should the polls prove true, Obama will lose around fifty-five seats in the House, and seven or eight in the Senate. Off no more than a gut feeling that some gap may have been closed in the past week, and that anger does not always make it all the way to the polling station, I will predict a loss of forty-five* in the House, and six in the Senate, and an unknowable capacity to regroup. And I will draw up a chair, and the popcorn, and watch the Republicans enter into full-scale civil war. But for all that, I wish that it was my party that was the one convening on hallowed battlegrounds, to dance and sing beneath the gold dome, of victory tomorrow.

*whoops.

12.

The Shellacking

The morning of election day I came back into Boston from seeing the Tea Party Express arrive at its final stop in Concord, New Hampshire. I had chosen Concord as a suitably portentous conclusion – the Tea Party rolling into the place where the Revolutionary War began, a final moment only slightly dimmed by the fact that there are two Concords, the Massachusetts one being the site of the famous battle. Damn pilgrims, and their woossy sentiments. My only hope is that the Tea Party Express, in choosing the place as their final stop, weren't labouring under the same misapprehension.

Back in Boston, I checked the DC party invite lists. A slot at the DNC party had come up. There was something at a human rights NGO, a friend was invited to a gathering of LGBT journalists, and a couple from bloggers encountered at the Wonkette pre-Sanity Rally party at The Big Hunt.

Barring extraordinary events, these would not be happy places, with the added advantage of work being practically impossible. There was also a Tea Party Patriots thing, but by then I'd had all the tea I could take. It seemed easiest to watch it all from the Harbourside Inn. That it was a stone's throw from the Old South Meeting House, where the original Tea Party had begun appealed to some sense of portentousness that was in me. As it turned out, of greater significance was that other site, that of the Boston Massacre.

Though the first results suggested that Democratic losses might not be as bad as first thought, with a uniform swing of only – only – six per cent, those hopes quickly came away. By nine-thirty eastern time, it was clear that the swing was heading to double figures, and the Democrats were taking one of the most serious beatings administered to any party in decades. The swing would ultimately be of the order of fifteen per cent on the 2010 vote.

In the House of Representatives, the Republicans would ultimately win sixty-four formerly Democrat seats, and lose three to them, for a net gain of sixty-one. The Democrats lost seats everywhere. In the South and Texas, they were chased out of their last remaining strongholds, losing three seats each in Tennessee and the lone star state, another three in Virginia, two in Mississippi, and others in Alabama, Arkansas, Georgia, Louisiana and the Carolinas. In the 'new West', two were lost in Colorado and Arizona, one each in New Mexico and Nevada. One each in Washington State, Idaho and Minnesota and the at-large districts in both the Dakotas as the north and plains collapsed in a wave. Five went in New York state, and even New England was not spared, with both New Hampshire districts going to the GOP. Actual gains were random and particular: the Delaware-at-large, Hawaii and one in Louisiana. More encouraging was the regions where they'd held the line – there were no losses in California or Oregon, five seats under threat in North Carolina were retained, as were three Iowa seats.

But this was small comfort for the greatest loss of all, the devastation across the Northeast, and in the perpetual swing state of Florida. From Pennsylvania through Ohio and Illinois to Michigan and Wisconsin, the Democrats were massively rejected: five in Pennsylvania, five in Ohio, three in the President's home state of Illinois, two in Michigan, Indiana and Wisconsin. Worst of all was Florida, where all four at-risk Democrat-held districts went; they didn't retain a single one. In some states, such as Pennsylvania, these results obscured the tough fight the Democrats had put up: the party retained as many at-risk seats as it lost. In others, such as Ohio, only one or two were retained. It was unquestionably a bloodbath.

Of course some of these districts were merely going back to the Republicans after two swings away from them in 2006 and 2008, as some commentator were every eager to point out. And observers from coming from polities using the Westminster system would be surprised to see such hysteria over around a seventh of the available seats changing hands. But of course that obscures two salient facts. The first is the iniquitous American system whereby political parties (at the state level) set the boundaries of congressional districts, thus generating a plethora of seats with weird and wonderful shapes – the windmill, the half-eaten pizza crust, the rabbit on a skateboard – that are effectively designed to be the permanent possession of one political party. The second is that, had the Democrats losses been limited to historically Republican seats that had despaired of the party in the mid 2000s, and/or swinging seats, the losses would have been of the order of thirty-five to forty-five. What should be alarming for the Democrats is that the extra tranche of seats included districts that had been Democrat for decades until the early Bush 43 years, taken a chance on the Republicans for a couple of terms, returned to the Democrats in 2006 or 2008, *and had now switched back to the GOP again*. This was especially so in the industrial north-eastern states that the Democrats hoped could be nailed down as solid blue entities for the foreseeable future: Pennsylvania, Michigan, Illinois and to a lesser extent Wisconsin. Coming in after the Bush administration had collapsed the economy and wrought devastation, these should have been dependable. Instead they are at the heart of the 2010 loss. Michigan's first and eighth districts, taking in a mixture of industrial, former industrial and rural areas, had been solidly Democratic since the 1940s – in the case of the first, since 1933. The third district in Pennsylvania, based around the tumbledown city of Erie had spent only six years under the Republicans between 1937 and 2002, when it went to the GOP for six years. Having come back in 2008, it has now gone away again. The eleventh district of that state, stretching through Wilkes-Barre and Scranton is perhaps the senior 'modern Democrat' district in the region having gone to the party in 1930, with only six red years in eighty. It has gone.

Other decades-long Democratic seats include the Illinois seventeenth, covering Moline, Springfield and other mid-size places – a significant loss because it was the proverbial 'rabbit on a skateboard', perhaps the most rococo gerrymandered district in the US. The fact that the Democrats can't hold onto a district which sneaks through the state practically house-to-house is a dire situation indeed. Other 'anchor' seats lost include the third district, in the south of Washington state, and the New Hampshire second, which had been in the Democratic camp for most of the past two decades.

One could look to other reasons for these sudden shifts, such as demographic change, geographical moves and the like. But had that been the case, there would have been more shifts towards the Democrats. But their only gains were anomalous – there was the Delaware-at-large, where the Tea Party had elevated Glen Urquhart as a companion to Christine O'Donnell, allowing the Democrats to run an end where their potential House rep was on film stating that the separation of church and state had been invented by Adolf Hitler. In Louisiana, Vietnamese-American Joseph Cao, elected in 2008 from an election with a hurricane-caused low turnout, was thrown out, and the first district in Hawaii returned after a brief dalliance with Republicans following a split Democratic vote in an earlier special election. Not one single vote represents a counter-trend that the Democrats could build on.

There was better news for the Democrats in the Senate, comparatively speaking. Six seats were lost – Arkansas, Illinois, Indiana, North Dakota, Pennsylvania, and Wisconsin. Each contest told a story. Pennsylvania was only briefly Democratic after Arlen Specter switched parties, and then lost nomination for the 2010 poll. In Arkansas, Blanche Lincoln had faced a union-funded primary challenge, after overdoing the cleave to the right, and lost any democratic base to speak of. In Illinois, Barack Obama's old seat was taken by a Republican, and in Wisconsin one of the most high profile liberal/radicals Russ Feinstein – co-author of the shredded campaign finance bill McCain-Feingold, and the only Senator to vote against the PATRIOT act – lost fairly heavily to a Tea Party endorsed candidate, Ron Johnston, with no public service experience, who avoided practically all press contact. Other Tea Party gains were in existing Republican seats – Florida, where Cuban-American Marco Rubio stormed to victory, Kentucky where 'aqua buddha' nudged Rand Paul to success, and Utah, where incumbent Bob Bennett had lost renomination to Mike Lee.

But the Tea Party was also responsible for several losses which could otherwise have been avoided. The most high-profile and expected was that of Christine O'Donnell, the one-time witch who had excluded former GOP congressman Mike Castle from a seat he would most likely have won. She went on to lose by seventeen per cent and true to form, gave a bizarre concession speech in which she claimed that 'this was a victory', urged her successful opponent to watch the half-hour video ad she had made and adopt her estate-tax abolition policy, before finishing with 'we've got a lot of food, we've got the room all night, so let's party!' You can take the girl out of Jersey, but she'll never get further than Delaware.

In Colorado, incumbent Democrat Michael Bennet narrowly held on against TP-endorsed challenger Ken Buck, the trend of the election overall suggesting a more moderate Republican candidate would have prevailed. Finally, in Alaska, the deposed Republican incumbent Lisa Murkowski appeared to have bested the Tea Party selected Joe Miller, in the first write-in campaign to succeed since the 1950s. Though Murkowski said she would caucus with the Republicans, victory as an independent suddenly gave her a lot more opportunity to deal with all comers.

Victory in these three races left the Democrats with fifty-three Senators, a sufficient margin to not only ensure victories in straight up-down votes, but to also ensure that the independent almost-Republican Joe Lieberman would not be in the tempting position of changing the balance of power by formally moving into the GOP caucus.

Throughout the night, the networks went to the Senate victory speeches, to gauge the mood of the future. Aside from the O'Donnell extravaganza, the winners all stuck to the script, a triumphalist trumpeting of the Tea Party's obsessions. In Kentucky, Rand Paul said that debt per se was evil, and that this departure from morality was the cause of America's current travails; in Florida, Marco Rubio thanked God for bringing him to America 'the only country in the world where your life isn't set down for you at birth', as people in Australia or Spain lived in feudal servitude. But the speeches everyone was waiting for were those from Nevada, for against all predictions Senate majority leader Harry Reid had prevailed against the high-profile Tea Party candidate Sharron Angle. Reid's political obituary had been read by everyone, save for the writer closest to the action – Jon Ralston of the *Las Vegas Sun*, who had observed the relentlessness of Reid's on-the-ground campaign, as well as the way in which Angle had alienated the Hispanic electorate, and predicted a Reid victory. Reid, when he rose to speak, had some of the pugnacity that must have once animated him as a young boxer – though in the end he still sounded like a mildly irritated episcopalian pastor who had misplaced his breviary. 'We haven't even begun to fight' he said. Grrrrr. Angle's 'concession' speech, by contrast, was pleasingly mad, the same trance-like insouciance that many of the Tea Party women have perfected. She talked about 'we the people' – the people being limited to those who had voted for her – bragged about the amount of out-of-state money she'd brought into the campaign, and free associated about how for the next six years they will keep Harry Reid honest, even though, should they cross the portal of his local office, the police will undoubtedly be called.

There were other close-run Senate races where the Democrats retained their hold. The most prominent of these was California, where the prominent liberal Barbara Boxer maintained a healthy margin of 9% over former Hewlett-Packard CEO Carly Fiorina. In Washington state, Patty Davis scored a narrow, hard-fought victory over Dino Rossi. And in West Virginia, Democrat John Manshin narrowly survived against out-of-state multimillionaire John Raese – effectively by going to war against his own party. In what most agree was the single most effective ad of the campaign, Manshin took a copy of the cap-and-trade climate change legislation, set it up on a stump, and shot it with a gun. The move appears to have dispelled any suggestions that he did not have the immediate interests of West Virginia at heart, and gave him the extra twenty-five he needed. But the Senate was the only bright spot for the Democrats all evening.

Perhaps worse than the House result was the state-by-state results. Key gubernatorial wins for the Republicans include Iowa, Michigan, Ohio, Oregon, Pennsylvania and New Mexico. Crucially, they also retained Florida in a narrow win. The Democrats won back California, with 70s governor Jerry Brown defeating Ebay billionaire Meg Whitman's $150m-plus self-funded campaign. But Republican gains also included a total of six hundred and eighty state house members – capturing eight.

Of the hundreds of propositions on state ballots, California's Prop 19 to legalise marijuana was defeated 55%-45%, but so too was a tripwire on its climate change act (it would have been suspended whenever unemployment rises above 5.5%). The attempt in Colorado to define a fetus as a legal person was heavily defeated. Medical marijuana was not permitted in Oregon and South Dakota, but may win in Arizona. Oklahoma banned the use not only of sharia, but all international law, in judicial proceedings, which suggested they would have problems making any habeas corpus rulings. It was a bad night also for the Blue Dogs – of the fifty or so in the caucus, fully half left Congress, either retired or defeated.

It was a shattering evening, with few high notes. Retaining the Senate was one, and the consequences of that victory may be momentous, especially if Supreme Court vacancies arise in the next two years. The speeches were another, with new Republican majority leader John Boehner repeatedly bursting into tears as he recounted the story of his own life, and the incomparable Christine O'Donnell telling her supporters – the people crowded behind her looking like a dinner-theatre cast of *Cabaret* – that 'we have won', and ending with the greatest concession speech line ever: 'we've got plenty of food and we've got the room all night!'.

Just before the coverage finished, I went out to the Seven Eleven to buy a couple of corn dogs. At the other end of Market Street was the Old South Meeting Place, where the Revolution had begun. Earlier I'd seen schoolkids re-enacting the meeting that led to the Boston Tea Party meeting. The performance had re-affirmed a basic sense that the politics and debates that had brought the revolution into being, mingled particular and universal themes, causes and passions in so complex a manner that nothing could be easily read off it. Yet somehow this mixture of natural rights, providentialism and mercantile tax avoidance had become a rallying point for the public face of the business class. And they had won. How had the Democrats let them take the mantle of audacity so easily? Was it their failure, or something deeper within American political life that meant that it would always so revert?

13.

Aftermath: The Crisis of American Liberalism

wednesday 3 november

The day after the election, President Obama gave a press conference, ahead of a trip to an official visit to India which presumably, for him, couldn't begin quickly enough. That morning, the new House majority leader John Boehner had addressed the media, his sunlamp tan glowing even more orange than usual (Obama, at the 2009 White House correspondents' dinner, had greeted him as a 'fellow man of colour'. 'Wassup John?' he had said gleefully). Now Boehner was back, with a vengeance. The North Carolinian – the glow tan gives him the hue of freshly-roasted tobacco – had a reputation as a crier, and he did not disappoint. As he spoke of the 'American Dream', his face began to tighten and his throat began to close. 'I know this is t...t...rer, true...(long beat) cos I've lived it.' A wobbly moment, before a return to calm? No, we were going to get the whole life story. Worked in my family's tavern, took every crappy job I could to get through college,' he sobbed. Had he been talking about someone else it would have been moving. That he was weeping over the epic quality of his own life gave it a self-pitying quality, less frontier than Oprah.

Senate minority leader Mitch McConnell was also there – furious that he had been denied equal billing by the failure to retake the Senate. McConnell was getting some stick for revealing that even taking responsibility for one branch of government hadn't dimmed the party's exclusively political focus, noting that the sole task for the next two years was to 'make sure that Barack Obama is a one-term President'.

President Obama, when he came out to speak early afternoon Wednesday, managed to please no one, as was becoming his signature. He spoke of the need to work together, and expressed hopes that the Republicans could do the same, which suggested to some that he hadn't switched on the news that morning. His later remarks – that this meant there would have to be more agreement as they pursued his programme together, suggested he hadn't watched it the night before either. Though he acknowledged that 'we got a shellacking', to both supporters and detractors alike, there seemed to be a curious disconnect from the political situation, a continuation of the attitude that had prevailed until well into the election campaign – a stubborn refusal to believe that actual politics would interfere with the administrative processes of government. Most people observed that Obama sounded tired, and perhaps it was a holding pattern. But it also sounded like the reality of a contrary process had suddenly hit, and a realisation of the threat it presented to such things as had been achieved.

By the time the President was winging his way to India – having avoided some holy site visits which would have obliged him to wear a turban – the discussion was already moving on, to some of the contradictions that Tea Party candidates would face, in particular the procedural raising of the official debt ceiling, which congress was required to pass by February 2011 in order to make ongoing loans servicing possible. Refusal of a rise, commentators warned, would throw US financial ratings, and the world economic system into fresh chaos. But the debt ceiling was standing at $14.3 trillion, and presented an obvious problem for Representatives and Senators-elect who had been elected on a platform of fiscal prudence. No matter what rationale you offered, fourteen and a half trillion was a hell of a blank cheque to put your name to. Rand Paul, whose opposition to debt was theological, was the first to say that he would consider filibustering the procedural raising of the ceiling. Later he clarified this to say that he would vote against the measure, but on the basis that others would pass it. Other Tea Party-endorsed candidates, such as Mike Lee in Utah, suggested they would demand large spending cuts as a condition of the vote, which offered the possibility of a showdown between Congress and the President. But it was not a showdown that progressives looked forward to with much enthusiasm. The President's willingness to compromise, his lack of enthusiasm for a political stoush – as demonstrated in his first post-election press conference – had persuaded many to quietly give up on him. Even on election night, many progressive commentators had started rubbing their hands at the prospect of the hard Right having to govern, and either make real cuts, or attach themselves to a fresh round of deficit spending. The mainstream Republican leadership already appeared to be stonewalling on election night, with Eric Cantor refusing to name a single program cut that the Republicans would advance in the new Congress.

The Left's gleeful anticipation of the trials of government upon the Tea Party may be vindicated, but it also appeared to be a rather desperate search for a silver lining. It also countenanced something that much of the Left had spent a lot of time denying during the campaign: that the Tea Party and others really cared passionately and only about small government and fiscal prudence, and would rapidly withdraw their support from any candidates who did not live up to that standard. Since they had instead argued that the Tea Party was motivated by baser notions, racist and otherwise, that government had been usurped by people who had no legitimate right to it, the sudden expectation of rationality was self-serving. The various people and groups who constituted the Tea Party had sat through the massive and insouciant build-up of deficits through the G.W. Bush years, just as earlier they had shown no great concern over Ronald Reagan's unprecedented deficit. In each case, the abstract concern about national finances had been wholly subsumed by the politics of identification and imagination – Reagan, and to a lesser extent Dubya, could project an image of American wholeness and exceptionalism that mad the deficit simply disappear from public consciousness effectively as a magician's misdirection, or Poe's purloined letter, hiding in plain sight. There was no reason to presume that it would necessarily go the other way this time round.

The Tea Partiers and the larger swathe of independent voters turning Republican had already shown themselves capable of impressive feats of cognitive dissonance – defending Medicare against the depredations of socialised medicine, blaming Obama for TARP, and much more. Quite possibly some of the more clear-headed and committed, those who had come from libertarian and Paulite groups, would turn their guns on a business-as-usual Republican majority, but many of the larger penumbra would simply fall into line, and ignore the GOP's continued enthusiasm for earmarks and entitlements – now reassured that American power was on the way to being returned into American hands. How much of that reaction to Obama and the Democrats is racist, consciously or otherwise, is impossible to know, and to suppose that it is stable over time is to assume too much. At the Tea Party Express finale in Concord, I spoke for ten minutes to a woman who argued cogently that Mitt Romney's use of an identical mandated health insurance plan to Obama's was acceptable because it was at a state level, and thus in line with the Constitution – and at the end of that she added, 'and I just think he's a Muslim and wasn't born in the US'. For a moment I thought it was amused self-parody for the media. But she was deadly serious. So I recategorised her in my head. Then her husband arrived and said hello. His name was Xavier. He was Mexican.

'This is a volatile time...they may change back' was the mantra recited by innumerable liberal commentators, taking a favourable lesson from the Democrats' short tenure in the House, 2006–2010, and the moonshine they had been promising a raddled and disappointed electorate. There was an element of desperation in this, and a refusal to recognise structural historical change. For sixty years, from the start of the New Deal to 1994, Congress had rarely, wholly departed from Democrat hands, and even the collapse of Southern hegemony in the Civil Rights era had not shifted that bias. By 1994, that had changed – the southern states had gone to the GOP, and the rust-belt states could not be counted as solid working-class votes. Though the Senate remained evenly split, it took twelve years and a disastrous Republican presidency for the Democrats to regain power in the House. Four years later it has returned to the Republicans with a majority that would take at least two elections to clear under the best of circumstances. In the Senate, narrow survival of a Democratic majority is mere prelude to a 2012 election in which twenty-four of the thirty-three Senate seats up for re-election are Democrat-held, virtually guaranteeing the loss of a majority.

The argument that the 2010 loss represented another episode in the volatility of the electorate could thus be seen as a way of masking the terrible truth – that the 1994 result represented the beginning of a new cycle in American politics in which Republicans would dominate Congress. By this reading, the 2006–2010 Democratic congress was an anomaly within this period, corrected by the 2010 election. This most recent election would thus be the commencement of a second wave of GOP dominance, potentially stretching well into the 2020s.

The simplest argument as to why this has occurred, from a progressive point of view, is that the Democrats didn't give its core constituencies enough reason to come out and vote for them. Despite the immediate flow of tax credit payments, provisions of the healthcare legislation and some job creation from the Recovery program, people weren't seeing the change they had demanded, especially in visibly lifting the country out of what was, in many regions, the beginnings of a depression.

However even if the will had been there to launch a new New Deal, both on the part of the administration and recalcitrant Blue Dogs, the haunting fear of the Democrats should be that they would still have been soundly defeated. Perhaps it is not merely that the Democratic base vote would not turn out for a midterm election, nor that a Republican base and variable independents had been motivated by a torrent of money supercharging a populist movement, but because the spirit of the age favours certain fundamental ways of doing politics that the Republicans have not only mastered but are predisposed to, and that Democrat are increasingly incapable of bodying forth. To put in a somewhat oversimplified form – American public life has gone backwards under the impact of slow but relentless historical decline, and the result has been a recrudescence, as people prefer myth over ideology, narrative over reason, fantasy to reality.

That the political leadership of the Obama administration and the Democrats appear to have had little idea that this was occurring and that it required a response at the same level, is perhaps the greatest condemnation of them that one could make. Having forged a potent myth to get Barack Obama first selected as the candidate and then elected – 'our time is now', 'we are the people we have been waiting for', a mix of civil rights prophesising, Alinskyesque community organising and a U2 lyric – they then abandoned the whole practice, and resorted to the driest technocratic rationalism, leaving a vacuum which the Right could fill with their own potent counter-myth. The Obama administration distanced itself at the same time as the Republicans climbed down from the neoconservative perch, and the dream of remaking the world, and directed their focus almost exclusively on the everyday details of American life.

This disastrous move is striking, incalculable in its effects, and telling. After the election of John F Kennedy, the left was outperformed in the creation of political myth all the way through to Obama – regaining power only when right-wing myths (Nixon's 'silent majority', Reagan's morning in America) had exhausted themselves. As the destruction of American workplaces, cities, towns and social networks had continued apace, such mythologising became more important than rounding up votes that had hitherto been dependent on rational class, area and group interest – and where a greater degree of rationality applied. The creation of 'Nixon Democrats' – white working-class people willing to vote against their own interests for reasons that were overwhelmingly cultural-political – helped start the process that would bring that politics to completion: the election of an administration willing to allow the dismantling of American industrial life, a process continued by every administration since (and recently, authoritatively documented in Judith Stein's *Pivotal Decade: How the United States Traded Finance for Factories in the Seventies*).

It has ultimately delivered an everyday life in which political and social frameworks have been smashed without new ones taking their place. The result is a failure of 'reality-testing' in areas where some ability to assess arguments is desperately necessary for people with no significant control over their own lives – arguments such as the revival of an economy via deficit reduction, for example. The Republicans told a simple tale over and over again – that a nation budgets like a family, and that running a deficit is the ultimate disaster. This struck many people as a wise and simple truth – even as they had no work due to the persistent underconsumption of the economy. Any number of answers could have been made to the Republican homily – that every family goes into debt to improve their lives (it's called a mortgage), or that a nation runs like a business, using debt strategically, or even that a nation simply isn't like a business, it's sui generis, and funds its own expansion by investment. Economists such as Paul Krugman and Robert Reich had been supplying arguments for months and years that put an alternative view as to how the economy worked. Obama and the Democrats never took it up. Instead they allowed the 'familial' myth of deficits to propagate relentlessly across the political sphere, until it had become the dominant myth of the election. Not only did this appeal to traditional (and illusory) notions of Republican financial competence, it connected to the lived experience of many people – trying to rein a debt-loaded budget for their own families, in tough times that would be exacerbated by the deflationary strategy that the Republicans were advocating.

What was truly brilliant about the Republican rhetorical strategy was that it connected this homily – the nation as family – to a deeper myth, that of the Constitution and American exceptionalism. The rhetoric of the Tea Party and its endorsed candidates connected the notion of familial life – don't spend more than you earn – with the surrogate family represented by the myth of America's founding. In this formulation, America's malaise originates out of a departure from the compact developed by the founders – a sin against the law laid down by the fathers, and transferred in its sacred documents. The myth offers a simple diagnosis for the country's current dilemmas, and one that also offers a solution through acknowledgement of guilt and the making of amends. It thus connects with the deep Puritan strands endemic to American political life – the notion that the good life comes from inner virtue, and that a good soul is what is most required. Such rhetoric appeals to deep places in the heart, because it not only offers an easy way to return things to rightness, it does so by vesting power in a higher authority – the ghostly authority of the founders who can grant absolution to their wayward successors. The one thing one is not required to do is face one's problems in a clear-eyed manner and solve them in the present moment.

In the 2010 elections, all of these themes came into view, like a shipwreck raised to the surface whole and entire. Of course it would be easy to take the constitutional rhetoric as irrelevant to most people's lives – and the Democrats unerringly did so. Once again they preferred an elite rationalism to a potent myth. After all, what did the stipulations of the Constitution matter to a family in Milwaukee that had suddenly seen its one pay cheque disappear? Nothing, except that as much as they were looking for a refloat, they were looking for a narrative that would explain why their lives had suddenly become so ill-favoured. Such a story – which offered that most important of commodities, social meaning – had a price above rubies. For every three people who would reject this as mystical bullshit, there would be one to whom this would, consciously or otherwise, find that it made sense at a deeper level. More importantly they would be more motivated to vote than those who saw nothing as offering any particular solution. What was perhaps most damaging for the Democrats was that the people that this myth was most likely to appeal to, were the same people to whom the Obama had appealed in 2008. Once you were in the market for a compelling story, its actual content was of less importance than that there was a myth.

The 'Tea Party myth' was absurd. Pumped and primped by big money and thinktank training, the minority of genuine libertarians and constitutionalists in the movement were swamped by those for whom the Obama administration was the existential equivalent of a persistent toothache, something they simply wanted removed. These were the ones would take any amount of nonsense from the GOP leadership, from FreedomWorks and the like, and would continue to line up for them whatever business-as-usual tricks they pulled, simply because they removed the notion that the Obama myth somehow represented one expression of the American spirit. Right from its

FOX-midwifed inception, liberals had discounted the Tea Party because of its transparently wilful quality.

But all myths are, at base, absurd. They project meaning onto an indifferent world, arising ab nihilo. What matters is whether they cut with the grain of the culture or not. There was little doubt that the capacity of the Republicans to sell a myth was in part derived from the more concrete world they inhabited. John Boehner's tears at his own hardly hardscrabble upbringing – before he entered the rarefied world of lobbyists and country clubs – may have been narcissistic and masturbatory, but they were also a measure of a world, that of service jobs and sales, that Democrats were increasingly isolated from. The progressive coalition had hitherto consisted of people with roots in local politics, union politics and a liberal intelligensia. Over the last three decades, the first of these two have fallen away, leaving only the last caste to dominate the party. These are people who live in a world of abstraction, policy and process – journalists, academics, policy officials, public servants, lifelong political professionals. They cannot believe the myth of the Constitution to which many of the Republicans subscribe – but what is more important they cannot subscribe to any myth. More exactly they commit to an anti-myth – that as long as they make people's lives incrementally and marginally better than their opposition, they will be politically favoured. Ostensibly this belief is a commitment to rationality – in fact it is an affirmation of elitism, an inability to see the great social divide between the rulers and the ruled, and the different modes of thought involved therein. The great fallacy of the elitists who now comprise the Democrats is that the mass of voters on whom they depend should not only be content with the top-down, and minimally advantageous, policies they determine for them, but should also think the way they do, in abstract and utilitarian rationalistic policy terms. Barack Obama's key advantage in besting Hilary Clinton was that he had seen through that delusion and offered them a myth in place of a demented obsession with nuts and bolts. Wisely, when faced with John McCain – a living myth – he had shifted to a different mode, but one also more congenial to his habitual style. It was then a style with which they became stuck, and when the appetite for myth resurfaced as the recession continued, they were unable to reclaim the territory.

The Democrats may well take endless comfort from the fact that they were outspent and out-organised by the post-*Citizens United* money - but the failed campaigns of Meg Whitman in California and Linda McMahon in Connecticut not only establish that vast amounts of money deliver diminishing returns (and at some point become counter-productive), they are also powerless against savvy thoroughly professional campaigns. But if they take from that ill-fortune the lesson that they were simply the victims of rotten luck, they will never find their way back to a winning strategy. What is most terrifying for those of us who believe that they are, on balance, the less worse option for America and the world, is that they appear to have learnt nothing from failures that now stretch back more than forty years, to the lost Humphrey–Nixon match of 1968. Throughout the 80s – Mondale and Dukakis – and Kerry in 2004, the Democrats put up essentially decent people hopelessly outmatched, and campaigns relentlessly outfooted not merely by low tactics but by appeal to gut instincts. Only with Bill Clinton, and then in a very different way Obama, did they manage to restore a mythical relationship to the average voter; albeit in very different ways: Clinton's very 90s 'I feel your pain', and Obama's minimalist message of 'hope'. The Democrats had a message of sorts – it was contained in their image of putting the car in the ditch and 'R' indicating the reverse drive – but even this one was abstract in itself. It was an allegory which had a pretty convoluted process of establishment. Though it was underused, it was the sort of thing more likely to appeal to someone who'd taken a course or two in John Milton than it would to Joe Sixpack.

By contrast, the Republicans' myth was supercharged in such a way that it could not only dispel earlier memories of failure, but take advantage of past transgressions. The notion that their own party had strayed from the true path could be easily folded into their myth of the Fall. They were the penitents who had learnt their lesson from recent failure and hubris; the Democrats were the ones who hadn't, yet, got it. More importantly, the Democrats hadn't understood the potency and particularity of the founding myth of America that conservatives attached to the Constitution. They thought, correctly, that only a very small number of people really obsessed about the Constitution; but they misunderestimated, as the man said, the way in which the fundamental myth of America would form an organising and energising principle for a much larger group of people.

Central to this myth was the special role that American exceptionalism plays in the cultural life of the nation. During the Bush era, sparked by the trauma of nine eleven and the remorseless rise of upstart nations like China and India, exceptionalism had become roaring back into the centre of American life. Though it had re-appeared in the Reagan years, even then it had been projected into the future as part of the final, and victorious struggle in the Cold War. When it returned in the Bush era, the concept had become almost fetishistic in its simplicity. Throughout the 2008 election, the question of American exceptionalism had arisen repeatedly amongst Republican candidates as a basic test. Barack Obama had dealt with the question by saying that he believed that America was exceptional for Americans just as England was exceptional for the English and so on – a cute formulation that managed to avoid the question entirely. By 2010 that would no longer do, and high-profile Republican candidates were outdoing themselves to affirm the unique nature of the United States. Sarah Palin had made it a centrepiece of her kinetic stump speech, and Tea Party endorsed candidates in particular competed to excel themselves in their commitment to the notion. Marco Rubio, in his victory speech, had echoed the extreme-exceptionalist notion of Daniel Webster that the US was a unique achievement in the history of the world, and the only place where enterprise and advancement was possible.

All patriotism involves, at its base, an irrationalism – an irrationalism that becomes more visible as people become more acquainted with other ways of life through travel and globalisation. Exceptionalism is easier to hold unselfconsciously in rising countries feeling their power – such as China – than in a country facing a transition to being one among many. But America's exceptionalism is, well, exceptional, in that it is founded on an ideas-based revolution, centred on a series of abstract texts, while nevertheless loaded with Christian ideas of providence and predestination. It thus presents itself as both a unique occurrence and an expression of universal human truth. It's a mix that is all the more intoxicating when all the evidence points to the opposite conclusion, and the recent flare-up of exceptionalism was not dissimilar to inflammation in a body – a last-ditch defence against infection, that nevertheless leaves it weakened. For these reasons, the liberals have never taken it seriously – indeed the failure of intelligent people to be able to take any strong form of exceptionalism seriously has become a selling point in its favour, for those who align themselves against the 'elites' and 'sophisticates'.

Several days after the election, the editor of *National Review Online*, Jonah Goldberg, asserted that 'America is the greatest country in the world. That doesn't mean it's perfect. But it is, and remains, the last best hope of Earth'. Despite having written one of the most asinine books of recent times in *Liberal Fascism*, Goldberg is no dummy, and it is signal that he had to assert his fidelity to exceptionalism despite all that could be said against it. Like creationism in the field of religion, exceptionalism had become a sort of political Kierkegaardian leap of faith: its very absurdity was a test to weed out the faithless. If you could withstand rational doubt about the notion that a middle-sized rebellious English colony which had solidified the 1688 Bill of Rights and gone on to substantial material success was 'the last best hope of man', then and only then could you call yourself a patriot.

Were American exceptionalism merely ridiculous – in the way that, say, remnant Portuguese exceptionalism is ridiculous – it could be easily dismissed. The trouble for progressives who had no regard for it was that American exceptionalism had enough of real distinctiveness to give it a residual energy that had the shape of an argument. This was easier to see from the farther, radical, Left than it was from the liberal Left, if only because one was less likely to be beholden to the notion of unquestioned political legitimacy than were liberals, and more sympathetic to the notion that the American revolution was a distinctive, though hardly unique, moment in human self-liberation. The Tea Party's appeal to the spirit of the revolution was always a little piss-weak: when one challenged them on the campaign trail as to whether and under what circumstances they would take the sort of audacious and voluntarist action ,that they had named themselves after. This usually prompted a rapid begging-off, which exposed the comprehensive incoherence of much of their position. Their media commentators were even better: one memorable broadcast had Charles Krauthammer praising the Tea Party to the skies, while tut-tutting about the militant action of French workers striking against the roll-back of their work conditions, 'I really think this is a mark of decadence'. But for all their dissembling, they couldn't take away from the fact that the revolution was a release of human energy and possibility, and was capable of generating energy and meaning even in the traduction of its memory.

Relatively uninterested in political myth, aware of the contradictory record of America in human affairs, and more interested in the general and universal features of modernity, the liberal-Left showed no interest in marshalling a counter-myth that would give an alternative account of what America was and could be. There were plenty of ways that that could have been done badly – getting into ridiculous arguments about the fourteenth amendment, for example. But part of setting an alternative agenda that could have helped carry some of its supporters to the polling booth and across the line, even in the face of a stalled and disappointing programme.

American liberals have watched the development of 'Americanist' fundamentalism on the Right for some time, with a great deal of bemusement and little affective understanding of its power. They have hoped that it would be of no consequence, and once it was clear that it was, that it would soon pass. Thus they have failed to develop an account of precisely how their philosophy and approach derives from traditions within American political life, and is part of it. The last progressive to really do this was FDR, and part of the problem with liberalism is that it has lived off the residual political capital of his monumental Presidency for so long that it cannot formulate a response to a movement that has claimed the mantle of radicalism as its own. Relaunching and regrounding liberalism in American terms is now an essential task. Perversely it was the victory of Barack Obama, with a substitute for an alternative philosophy, that delayed for a time the need for that essential work. There is something bizarre about a President whose past job was as a professor of constitutional law being blindsided by a constitutional fundamentalism that lacks even a skerrick of internal consistency.

The power of the ideas being put out by the Tea Party, and Godfather figures such as Dick Armey, was the way in which it joined technical economics – minimal taxation and the small state – to an all-inclusive philosophy of human life, as vested in a national tradition. Such a politics has never taken root in Europe, the commonwealth or the developing world because it can never rise above the level of technique and means; in the US it is means and end, immanent meaning. Unless it is met with an alternative way of thinking about American life, the nation's politics will always relapse to this default setting. Battling toe-to-toe with constitutional fundamentalism is not an intellectual luxury for American progressivism, it is a first, essential step to political parity.

What would such a fightback look like? Surely it begins with a notion of what America is, a living nation. The idea of the Constitution as some inviolable document is at obvious variance with its history – the damn thing was only ratified by a number of states on the understanding that it would be immediately amended, with what became the Bill of Rights. Encoded within its ratification is the notion that each generation would deal with the unique circumstances presented to it by history, by reinterpreting and adding to its founding principles. Any other approach to national politics subordinates present life to past vitality, a process that privileges the dead over the quick and tends towards ancestor worship. The bias towards the present rather than the past was the centrepiece of FDR's invocation of 'having nothing to fear but fear itself', identifying conservatism as ultimately inimical to the human spirit of remaking our world through our own present capacities, and braving the possibility of uncertainty and failure. One reason why the conservatism of the Tea Party has such energy, compared to the often visible defeat, doubt and fatigue of liberal standard-bearers, is that it presents a counterfeit radicalism in which the success of bold action is guaranteed by fealty to a document of supernatural origins. FDR's further advancement of the 'four freedoms' was, as we have seen, even more audacious, since it advanced two positive freedoms – from want, and from fear – that the Constitution did not recognise at all. That negative and positive freedoms can ultimately come into contradiction was frequently thrown at the New Deal did not matter a whit – it was an all-encompassing progressive philosophy of action which expressed itself in vernacular American terms, and put its opponents on the defensive.

Had the Obama administration done this from the start, and used such a comprehensive approach to maintain a mobilised and organised mass base, it would be in a vastly better position than it is now. Is there any possibility that such an approach would be revived in the remaining two years before the 2012 poll? There is no barrier to it, save the disposition of team Obama itself, and the political personality of the President. Elite figures oriented to the control of the masses rather than the representation of them, they are permanently divided within themselves, as regards populist causes such as free trade versus national development and protection, and strengthening labour's conditions via control of immigrant labour supply. One sees this again and again in interviews and TV debates, where conservatives regularly walk all over liberals, because the latter are unable to have a full-throated defence of popular causes, much less to turn them into a more general philosophy, expressed in a concrete and mythologised form. By contrast John Boehner can unselfconsciously present himself, tear-stained, as the living embodiment of what he believes, revelling in the full absurdity of it. The left produces few progressive populists and those that do emerge – Michael Moore is one recent example – are kept at arm's length. Whatever strategies team Obama come up with in the next months, they are unlikely to travel down this path.

Indeed it may be that progressivism will not return to this full-blooded philosophy until it, and the country, has met with fresh disaster and has nowhere else to go. It is impossible for a mainstream party not to work for its own success, but the best that the Democrats can realistically hope for in 2012 is retention of the Presidency against a hostile Congress. Four more years – of defensiveness, gridlock, and compromise, with a repeat of the past political cycle. The Democrats will take the blame for meagre achievements, while the GOP will cleave to an ever-greater American fundamentalism, even as they conspire in fresh rounds of deficits, earmarks and stasis. Perhaps that will discredit them. It is far from certain. And perhaps what is required of progressives is the courage of a longer game. Maybe the only thing that will make a genuine progressive political advance possible is a Republican grand slam in 2012 or 2016, giving them unbridled opportunity to put their magical thinking into practice, to finally establish that nothing, not even the Constitution, will save the country from dealing with the challenges and demands of a changing and multipolar world with all the resources, ingenuity and dynamism of a living people.

November 12, 2010.

Endnotes

chapter 2: tea partying in delaware with the white witch

p. 26 The Harry Reid–Sharron Angle contest was extensively covered in 'Desert Storm' by Nicholas Lemann, *The New Yorker*, p.57, 25.10.10

chapter 6: obama nirvana in seattle

p.51 Karl Rove, 'Signs of the democratic apocalypse', *Wall Street Journal*, p.A15, 28.10.10

p.51 NYT/CBS poll, quoted in *New York Times*, p.A16, 28.10.10

p.61 Karl Rove quoted in Frank Rich, 'The Grand Old Plot Against The Tea Party', *New York Times*, op-ed, 31.10.10

chapter 8: leaving new haven

p.73 Bob Herbert, 'The Corrosion of America', *New York Times*, op-ed 26.10.10

p.74 *Australian Financial Review*, 05.11.10

chapter 9: the suburbs of providence

p.82 'Obama success outweighed by job losses', *New York Times*, 27.10.10

chapter 10: this is a sign about nothing

p.85 Maureen Dowd, column, *New York Times*, 31.10.10

p.91 *Tea Party Nationalism* by Devin Burghart, Leonard Zeskind, published by NAACP and Institute for Research & Education on Human Rights.

chapter 11: the tea party express rolls home

p.94 Ed Pilkington, 'Amy Kremer takes her Tea Party express from coast to coast', *The Guardian,*18.10.10

p.96 Keli Carender, interview, 23.10.10

chapter 12: the shellacking

p.107 Jon Ralston, 'Atmospherics are terrible for Reid, but he will hold on', *Las Vegas Sun*, 31.10.10

chapter 13: aftermath: the crisis of american liberalism

p.110 'Dems rip McConnell's "one-term" remark' *Washington Post*, 27.10.10

p.115 Judith Stein, *Pivotal Decade: How the United States Traded Finance for Factories in the Seventies*. Yale UP, 2010

p.121 Jonah Goldberg, 'Liberals insist on bashing American exceptionalism', 'The Corner', *National Review Online*, 13.11.10

p.122 Charles Krauthammer, 'Ah Voters Must Be Deranged' syndicated op-ed column , accessed at *Charleston Daily Mail*, 23.10.10

Appendix

The 2010 Midterm Elections

Total votes:
Republicans 43,879,934 – 52.2%. share gain on 2008: 9.7%
Democrats 37,492,325 – 44.6% share drop from 2008: 8.6%

The 111th Congress (2009-2010)
The House of Representatives: 255 Democrats, 178 Republicans, 2 vacancies (as of June 14, 2010).
   Majority: Democrats, 77

Senate: 57 Democrats, 2 independents (caucusing with Democrats), 41 Republicans.
   Majority: Democrats, 19

Elected to 112th Congress (2011-2013)
House of Representatives:
240 Republicans, 189 Democrats, six yet-to-be-decided**
   Majority: Republicans, 61 to 67

Senate: 51 Democrats, 2 independents (caucusing with Democrats),
46 Republicans, 1 independent (caucusing with Republicans)*
   Majority: Democrats, 6

Republican gains, by region

(districts with no voting history are swing districts; 'Democrat 19XX-19XX' indicates a district held by that party for more than 90% of the period cited)

<u>New England:</u>
New Hampshire 1 (east)
New Hampshire 2 (west)
(entire state)

<u>New York state, and mid-East coast</u>
New York 13 (Staten Island) (Democrat 1911-1993)
New York 19 (NYC suburbs Democrat 1933-93)
New York 20 (rural east, Democrat 1933-93) (BD)
New York 24 (mid-state, mixed) (BD)
New York 29 (south-west, mixed)

New Jersey 3 (urban, mid-state)
Maryland 1 (east Chesapeake, urban) (BD)

Upper South
Virginia 2 (peninsula and coast) (BD)
Virginia 5 (mid state, Democrat 1889-2000)
Virginia 9 (west, rural)
North Carolina 2 (mid-state, Democrat since 1900)

Rust-belt and North-East
West Virginia 1 (north, rust-belt)
Pennsylvania 3 (Erie, Democrat 1953 – 2003) (BD)
Pennsylvania 7 (urban, mid-state)
Pennsylvania 8 (urban NE) (BD)
Pennsylvania 10 (rural north, usually Republican) (BD)
Pennsylvania 11 (mid state, urban, Democrat since 1954)

Ohio 1 (urban west)
Ohio 6 (mixed, eastern edge) (BD)
Ohio 15 (urban, mid-state, Republican)
Ohio 16 (urban mid-state, mainly Republican)
Ohio 18 (east mid-state, mixed) (BD)

Indiana 8 (west, urban) (BD)
Indiana 9 (south-east mixed, Democrat since 1965) (BD)

(Illinois 8 – yet to be declared)
Illinois 11 (urban, eastern mid-state, Democrat 1961 - 1996)
Illinois 14 (urban, mid-state, Republican)
Illinois 17 (urban, western edge, Democrat since 1983)

Wisconsin 7 (northwest, rural, Democrat since 1969)
Wisconsin 8 (northeast, mixed)

Michigan 1 (north, rural, Democrat since 1933)
Michigan 7 (south, mixed)

North and Great plains
Minnesota 8 (east, rural, Democrat since 1947)
North Dakota-at-large (mixed, Democrat since 1981) (BD)
South Dakota-at-large (BD)
Idaho 1 (urban, west, mainly Republican) (BD)

Midwest
Missouri 4 (west, mid-state, rural, Democrat since 1935)
Kansas 3 (urban, east) (BD)

West
Nevada 3 (Las Vegas suburbs)
Colorado 3 (west, urban) (BD)

Colorado 4 (east, urban, Republican since 1973) (BD)
Arizona 1 (mixed, north-east, R since 1953)
Arizona 5 (Phoenix suburbs, Republican 1985-2006) (BD)
New Mexico 2 (southern, urban, Republican since 1981)

<u>West Coast</u>
Washington 3 (north west)
(California 11 – yet to be declared)
(California 20 – yet to be declared)

<u>South, Texas and Florida</u>
Louisiana 3 (south, urban, Democrat 1885-1995) (BD)
Mississippi 1 (north, rural, Democrat 1873 – 1995) (BD)
Mississippi 4 (southwest, mixed) (BD)
Arkansas 1 (east, mixed, Democrat since 1875) (BD)
Arkansas 2 (midstate, urban, Democrat since 1875)
Alabama 2 (east, mixed, Republican since 1965) (BD)
Tennessee 4 (midstate, rural, Democrat since 1871) (BD)
Tennessee 6 (north-central, rural, Democrat since 1843) (BD)
Tennessee 8 (northwest rural, Democrat since 1875)
Georgia 8 (midstate, urban) (BD)
South Carolina 5 (north central, Democrat since 1839)

Texas 17 (east, midstate, Democrat since 1919)
Texas 23 (south west, Mexican border, rural)
Texas 27 (south east coast, Democrat since 1983)

Florida 2 (panhandle, urban, Democrat since 1889) (BD)
Florida 8 (central peninsula, urban)
Florida 22 (urban, south coast peninsula)
Florida 24 (urban, northeast)

**

Democratic gains: 3

Delaware-at-large (urban, Republican since 1993)
Hawaii 1 (Honolulu, Democrat since 1971)
Louisiana 2 (New Orleans, Democrat since 1891)

Senate

<u>Republican pickups:</u>
Arkansas
Pennsylvania
Illinois
Indiana
Wisconsin

North Dakota

At-risk Democratic holds:
Colorado
California
Connecticut
Delaware
Nevada
Washington
West Virginia

Safe Republican holds:
Alabama, Alaska, Arizona, Florida, Georgia, Idaho, Iowa, Louisiana, Kansas, Kentucky, Missouri, New Hampshire, North Carolina, Ohio, Oklahoma, South Carolina South Dakota, Utah

Safe Democratic holds:
Maryland, New York (2 seats), Oregon, Vermont.

Gubernatorial

Republican gains
Iowa
Kansas
Maine
Michigan
New Mexico
Ohio
Oklahoma
Pennsylvania
Tennessee
Wisconsin
Wyoming

Democratic gains
California
Connecticut
Hawaii
Vermont

Independent
Rhode Island (from Republican)

*presuming that Lisa Murkowski wins as write-in candidate. In either case, the seat stays in Republican hands

**as of November 12, 2010